TOMORROW – WHO KNOWS?

TOMORROW – WHO KNOWS?

Alma and Ray Moore

ARROW BOOKS

Arrow Books Limited
20 Vauxhall Bridge Road, London SW1V 2SA

An imprint of Random Century Group

London Melbourne Sydney Auckland Johannesburg
and agencies throughout the world

First published in Great Britain by
Constable and Company Limited 1989
Arrow edition 1990

Printed and bound in Great Britain by
Courier International Ltd, Tiptree, Essex

ISBN 0 09 974650 6

Contents

FOREWORD
by Lynda Lee-Potter   9

PART ONE
Alma's Story   27
Chapter one   29
Chapter two   46
Chapter three   59
Chapter four   77
Chapter five   90
Chapter six   101
Chapter seven   114

PART TWO
Ray's journal   127

EPILOGUE
by Alma Moore   165

Acknowledgements   167

FOR RAY

Well, I know someday
This precious dream will have to end,
But I want you to know
It was oh so very good, my friend.
And though the magic may all fade away
We will live and love today,
For tomorrow – who knows?
Yes, tomorrow – who knows?

ALMA

List of Illustrations

First Plate Section

Alma and her sister Audrey King
Alma's parents
Alma aged 14, with her family
Ray's family
Ray and his father
Alma and Kathy Taylor
Alma and her first husband
Charlie Dawson and Alma
The young Alma King with Roy's pride and joy
The BBC Manchester Annual Dance
Ray broadcasting
The honeymoon in Jersey
Ray at the the start of his professional career
Alma in her composing days
The studio – Ray's second home
Ray auditioning for newsreader at the BBC
ATV Birmingham
The French singer Minouche and Ray in Monte Carlo
Terry Wogan and Ray

Second Plate Section

Ray with Vic Damone and Charles McClelland
Pop Score – the 200th programme
Ray with the Salvation Army
Radio 2 – bright and early
Ray at Christmas
Ray trying to look like an old Spaniard
Ray signing for his fans
Ray and his god-daughter

Alma sorting out requests for Children in Need
In Stratford-upon-Avon, 1987
About to leave for the Charity in Concert version of *Mack and Mabel*
On board the France-England car ferry
Making a home movie
0530-ish on the Bog-Eyed Jog in Birmingham
Getting ready for the London to Brighton race
Lovely Ray in a field of poppies
Ray enjoying a relaxing sail during Cowes Week
Ray on a walking holiday in Devon
At Cherry Cottage

Third Plate Section

Julie Pearce and Ray
On a promotion trip for British Rail
Walking the London Marathon course
An early morning live interview with Eddie Large
Ray with Syd Little and his wife
Ray, Denis O'Keeffe and Johnny Roadhouse on a Bog-Eyed Jog
Outside broadcast in Deptford
At Manor House Hotel
Janet Moore, Mrs Moore and Mrs King
Alma and Julie at Julie's Dad's wedding
Ray, Alma and Paul
Julie, David and Ray registering for the 100 mile walk
Ray signing his autobiography, with Alma and John Wilcox
Outside Sherratt and Hughes during a signing session
Ray with 'Management'
Ray's last gig
Noel Edmonds with Alma
Ken Bruce accepting the Gold Badge of Merit Award on behalf of Ray

Foreword

by

LYNDA LEE-POTTER

I first got to know Ray Moore in exactly the same way as nearly five million other listening strangers who thought of him as a brilliant, wise and much loved friend.

Driving to work at dawn, through the country lanes, I switched on my car radio every weekday morning at 5.30 to hear that husky, mesmeric, spellbinding voice. It was a voice honed to perfection on too many cigarettes, too much Beaujolais and a lifetime of late nights. Because Ray was not a moderate man. If he were talking passionately with friends in the early hours he never wanted the night to end. He was not a host who would ever put the cork back in a bottle of red wine. He and his wife Alma were the last to leave any party.

Ray always had a premonition that he would die whilst he was still young and it was as though he wanted to live two days for every single one he spent on earth, to extract every possible ounce of laughter, joy and fun, to relish every waking moment. When he worked through the night, as he frequently did, he absolutely hated to go to bed even for a mere couple of recuperative hours in daylight. He felt life was for living not sleeping. And he lived his life with so much intensity, it's scarcely surprising that the song he loved more than any other and which was sung at his memorial service, was that show stopper from *La Cage Aux Folles*, 'The best of times is now, is now, is now'.

He was quite simply the finest, most innovative broadcaster of his day, one who was prepared to take risks. 'There's no script,' he said to me once. 'I write down a few key words before

I start, then I'm flying. I still get nerves, not fear, but panic, excitement. I like danger. I don't want a safe show, I want the listener to be challenged, stimulated, I want things to swerve all over the place. I do it all on coffee and adrenalin. There's just me and an engineer. A live microphone for two hours is kind of awesome. The dark hours are more intense than daytime, communicating late at night or early morning you can feel the electricity. Radio can spot a phoney at a hundred yards. Radio is a much more subtle business than television. I can sense the listeners out there, it's almost tangible.

'It takes me an hour or two to come down to earth afterwards. I feel I've been with good, warm friends. I always say goodbye privately to everybody when I'm off air, I feel it's been that intimate and personal. And as with good friends, sometimes they're a bit depressed. I just hope I can raise a wry grin from people where before there's been a frown. At the end I just disappear like a Cheshire cat. I might say, "Be careful when you go out, it's cold, put your woolly on," as you would to a friend. Sometimes there's a psychic kind of feeling. It's difficult to explain but it's close to lunacy. Some days I come off air and I want to shoot myself. Other times I'm intoxicated with euphoria, I've seen glimpses of the mountain top.'

Ray had absolutely no conception of the mammoth effect he had on people's lives until ironically the Ray Moore show was over forever. It was only when the news that he had cancer of the mouth was announced in all the newspapers on January 30th that he realised how important he was to millions. The story was headlined in nearly every newspaper in the land and grieving letters by the sackful poured into the BBC. 'We've designated today for crying, tomorrow we'll laugh,' he said.

Listeners were totally desolated, it was as though a member of their own family had been given a sentence of death. Because they knew I'd interviewed him many people wrote to me, desperate to share their emotional trauma, heartbreak and sense of loss. In all my years in journalism, I have never ever known such passionate sense of involvement and my office was literally overwhelmed with thousands of letters. They included one from a woman who said, 'When my husband died I was devastated and found waking in the morning the hardest and loneliest time. Dear Ray has given me the strength and courage to get on with my life.' His power actually was as stupendous as that and another listener wrote, 'I can tell you, it's practically been nonstop crying when I think of his sheer bloody bravery in carrying on, keeping it a secret for so long and knowing we won't hear those lovely deep rich tones and gentle wit any more in the mornings . . .'

Ray wasn't just another talented broadcaster. People grieved for him as though he were one of their own. The most extraordinary thing is that although he had these staggering listening figures for such an anti-social hour, nobody had actually realised how adored he was. As Terry Wogan said at his memorial service which was full of eulogies, 'It's a crying shame that all the people who love, admire and cherish Ray Moore now that he's gone, didn't make more of a fuss of him when he was alive and kicking and broadcasting like a good'un. Why did he never win any of the glittering prizes? He was too ill to broadcast when he won his first award. I know he's enjoying this today. But I also know he would have enjoyed a bit more fuss and palaver, when he was alive. Ray Moore got bypassed more often than Kingston but it didn't embitter him or, if it did, he kept it to himself. He was a pro you see. He knew how good he was and he knew that what he did he did better than anybody else.'

The words were part of a long, loving tribute from Terry which was characteristically warm and witty. He intended to make us laugh because that is what Ray would have wanted. But after the memorial service was over, the congregation went back to the BBC for a glass of wine and told him how much in fact he'd made us cry. We cried because to hear one consummate broadcaster talking about another with such admiration, respect and affection was deeply moving. And we cried because what he said was true. Ray did have to die before he was publicly extolled, praised to the skies and finally treated by the BBC like the glorious communicating star he was. Few BBC performers can have had a more spectacular memorial service than that which was broadcast live from All Souls Langham Place on 3rd March 1989. The celebration ended with a thundering, stupendous rendering of 'The Best of Times is Now', played and sung by the Salvation Army songsters, the BBC Singers and the Syd Lawrence Orchestra. Never before can there have been such tumultuous applause in church. We'd been told that we were allowed to clap but there could have been no stopping us. The general feeling was that Ray was looking down on the whole show from some little nook and cranny with his famous grin, beating time to the music and tickled pink by all the fuss.

It was certainly lovely to hear him praised by the famous. Previously we'd all thought that he was our own personal discovery, that few other people were daft enough to be up and wide awake at 5.30 in the morning listening to a comic genius. He spun a magic kind of gossamer web around the country, enchanting and encompassing insomniacs, night shift workers, newsagents, journalists, the sad and sundry and the lonely.

'If you're on your own,' he said one Christmas 'I'll be your friend.' And he literally was a dear and valued friend to an army of people he never met. In the days of television the strength of radio is sometimes overlooked but in many ways it is a far more powerful medium. The tie between broadcaster and listener is more personal, intimate and stronger, bringing friendship and light where perhaps there was loneliness. Long before I met him I thought of Ray Moore, as indeed did all his listeners, in a proprietorial sort of way. I suspect we all believed we were the only ones clever enough to have discovered him. It was only when I wrote about him for the first time that I realised what a bond it was being a Ray Moore listener. Nobody who loved him could be all bad and, as one *Daily Mail* reader said in a letter, 'I've never been able to stand you. But now that I know you're a Ray Moore fan, I'm beginning to think you can't be as awful as I thought'.

I met him face to face for the first time, in October 1987, when I interviewed him over lunch at London's Savoy Hotel and he was as lovely and eccentric as I'd imagined. His inventive, wondrous flights of fancy on his programme were once described memorably by the highly esteemed critic Nancy Banks-Smith. 'Moore comes from a long line of wooden legged greengrocers and short sighted undertakers,' she wrote in the *Guardian*. 'His father used to take him to school in the hearse. Listeners sometimes, though not often, request a moving poem about Moore senior's myopia which he delivers in a monochrome chant . . . My father had a rabbit and he thought it was a duck. So he put it on the table with its legs cocked up . . . He will sing you "Mersey Dock and Harbour Board" to the tune of Mersey doats and dozy doats if you're not careful. Like all Liverpudlians, he lives on the other side of a distorting mirror where nude ballooning is all the rage or, if you don't have the figure for it, single-handed round the world golf. Familiar buildings and singers emerge slightly askew as in the Royal Halibut Hall and Julio Double Glazing Arse. He seems to live in the plaintive hope of meeting Frank Sinatra who never answers his letters.'

It was a brilliant pastiche of his wondrous surrealist flights of fancy which he once called 'a distillation of the glorious soup of knowledge in my head'. Every morning he created especially for us a kind of Liverpudlian Alice in Wonderland backcloth where

[15]

the bizarre and eccentric were commonplace and totally to be expected.

'I'll have a cigarette and a mouthful of red wine,' he said to me in the Savoy's River Restaurant as he reminisced about his rather harsh childhood and about meeting his beloved Alma. When we finally left, the waiters were taking the cloths off the tables, it was nearly 5 o'clock and the lamplights were shining over the Thames.

We talked about what a glorious professional year it had been for him, about his forthcoming sponsored jog in aid of the Children in Need appeal. He seemed such a golden, blessed man, approaching the peak of a glittering career, doing a job he adored, married to a wife he loved so much she almost seemed part of his soul. Men who are deeply in love with their wives can't help bringing them into the conversation and there were endless anecdotes about 'Management' as she became known to listeners or 'Big Alma' as Terry Wogan once christened her. She did indeed get lots of letters from fans beginning 'Dear Management'. It conjured up a rather large, bossy matriarchal figure but in truth she's tall and elegant with a stunning figure and endless legs.

'She's the strong one,' Ray insisted, 'I'm very emotional, I cry a lot. Alma says, "Not the bloody waterworks again. Call yourself a man?"' It wasn't of course as simple as that and Alma drew as much strength from her husband as he did from her.

He talked of how the previous week he had walked the eight miles home from Broadcasting House to Blackheath, in the aftermath of the 1987 hurricane which blocked nearly every London street with fallen trees. He looked tanned and remarkably fit and I thought only that he was lovely, joyous, uniquely happy and very lucky because he had a rare, totally original talent and he was using it to enrich people's lives. I had absolutely no conception that he knew he was dying, that his broadcasting

[16]

days were over, that he realised his death might be slow and terrible, as the cancer ate away his face. I didn't know then, that within a year the mellifluous voice would become almost unintelligible, except to Alma who could always understand what he meant. I didn't know that only two months previously he'd been to see a cancer specialist, who had told him that he wouldn't be able to carry on working much longer than the following February, and that he probably had only two more years left to live. The forecast was pretty accurate because Ray Moore did his last broadcast on Thursday January 28th 1988. He refused the instant, drastic surgery which might have kept him alive marginally longer, but which would have destroyed any quality of life and he never regretted this decision.

He told few people that he was ill and because they didn't know he was able to forget it intermittently himself. I truly believe he enjoyed our Savoy lunch, that he was able to relish the moment, the wine, the delicious food and enjoy it, as he enjoyed everything all his life with tremendous zest, concentrating powerfully on now.

Alma found the situation much harder to bear when other people still didn't realise how ill he was. There were lots of jokes about the beard he'd grown to hide the lump which was getting larger every day. Ray however felt that if nobody knew about the cancer, then the whole black, unbelievable awfulness might just go away.

He was a highly intelligent, creative, widely read man but there was still a touch of wide-eyed wonderment about him. Even when he was hugely successful, and the Ritz became like a second home, there was still a little bit of Ray that never got over the awe of feeling 'Here I am, Ray Moore from Liverpool, sitting with a glass of champagne in this posh hotel'. He never became blasé or arrogant, which is why his broadcasting never became slick, bland or glib. He just quietly went along doing superb programmes, acknowledged by other broadcasters as the best in the business.

Incredibly he was overlooked by the BBC, when Terry Wogan left his famous morning slot to do Wogan on television three times a week. There were continual stories of an endless search for a successor, when they had the ideal person already sitting in Broadcasting House. Ray was hurt that he was never asked to take over the prestigious, later slot which would have given him a new audience, but he was not a man to make an outraged fuss. Fundamentally he knew, albeit without vanity, how very good he was and he was never prepared to hustle or jostle for position. It was an amalgam of both pride and humility. It was why he could talk to rich and poor, old and young, why even at the height of his fame he could walk into a backstreet pub in Liverpool and still be treated as a mucker not a star.

He and Alma used to love to meet at the Ritz before they went to the theatre, and after his death Alma received a sweet note from the manager saying how they would all miss him. Even when he was beginning to feel a sense of debilitating tiredness in the winter of 1987 he still insisted on touring the country before Christmas raising £100,000 for the BBC's Children in Need appeal.

After the illness was diagnosed, he was able to do his beloved programmes for nearly six more months. One can only hazard a guess at the bitter sweetness of the emotions he must have felt, sitting in the studio in the early mornings, and in my opinion those programmes were the finest he ever did. But when he listened back to one of the tapes in his final week, he felt that his voice was beginning to slur and he told the BBC that he would have to leave. He passionately wanted to do one more programme, knowing that it would be his requiem. They refused to allow it. I suspect, however, that if he had been given the opportunity, he would have achieved the seemingly impossible and done a supremely professional show. He would not have made any emotional farewell, but just slipped away, like a friend who'd soon be back, as he had done for nearly a decade at 7.30 every morning. We'd have listened with joy as we always did, laughed out loud, said, 'Oh Ray is a card, isn't he?' and we would not have had the remotest idea that we were listening to a man whose heart was breaking.

The illness struck when he was approaching the height of his career, when widespread recognition for his magical, formidable talents had finally arrived and he seemed to be on the brink of having everything he'd ever yearned for. When I look back on our first meeting, I can only marvel at his valour. Four months later, as you will read in this book, BBC publicist Sandy Chalmers rang me up to tell me that Ray Moore's broadcasting career was over, that the mellifluous beautiful voice would slowly be silenced until he could speak no more. She said that he would be happy to talk to me. We did an interview on the telephone and I was the one who wept. Through that terrible, endless day, when his life was disintegrating, he somehow found the reserves of strength to be endlessly polite to journalists.

'You keep whistling in the dark, praying and hoping it will go away,' he said to me, 'but there is no point in beating about the bush, the doctors have told me it's incurable. This is the saddest day of my life but I didn't want to put the BBC in the position of saying, "Hang on son, you're not as good as you were." I think the decision to quit now is right, rather than dribbling on with people asking "Is he drunk or drugged?" I'd rather leave you wanting more. I listened to a recording of one of my broadcasts earlier this week, which I haven't done for many months, out of fear probably, and it was worse than I'd suspected. I thought, "The game is up." I was in two minds whether I should tell you about the cancer when we had lunch last year. But there was a sort of shame attached to it.'

Guilt about his lifetime of drinking and smoking tortured him for a period and he said once to Alma, 'God must be saying "Laddie I gave you this wonderful talent and you blew it."' Alma told him passionately, 'No Ray, God gave you this wonderful talent and look how you've used it'.

In all the best marriages, husbands and wives enhance each other. They expand and blossom under each other's influence and Alma and Ray were the personification of this. In the final year of his life, they shared a world that was full of both laughter and tears. The two emotions probably summed up their whole relationship, from the day they first set eyes on each other in an office at Broadcasting House in Manchester and were instantly and equally, struck by a *coup de foudre*. They both always felt that it was predestined they should fall in love. They believed there was a formidable force at work ensuring that they should make their lives together, even though when they met Alma was married with a seven year old son, David.

Today that small boy is thirty-one, a successful surveyor and development consultant, running his own business. He is loving, supportive, proud and deeply protective of his mother, which speaks volumes for her, for David and for his own father Roy who brought him up. It's also a tribute to Ray who couldn't have loved David more if he'd been his own. 'More than a father' were the words on the wreath from David at Ray's funeral. It was David who slept on a mattress on the floor next to Alma, the night after Ray died. It was David who stood next to Alma in Blackheath church on the day of the funeral. And when the funeral was over, when Ray's friends had wept and laughed and reminisced, it was David who ordered the first bottle of champagne, because that's what Ray would have done. Alma left her home and security, the safe, the known and her child because of the intensity of the emotions she felt for Ray. She then went back to her son and husband, because everybody involved was paying a terrible price for her obsession with a man nine years younger than herself. She had to go back to him however for the simple reason that she could not bear to be without the young broadcaster she loved beyond any sense of self-preservation.

When Ray became ill, he said to her on a particularly black day, 'Were we right to go off together? Now you're having to look after me in this condition?' And Alma said, 'Perhaps it's why it's all happened, because I've got the strength to look after you, to pull you through'.

She's a lovely, warm-hearted, outgoing person who cares very much what people think of her. And today, the memory and guilt and shame of those terrible days, when she left David, remain vividly with her. She still finds it traumatic to recall them and I know that she has wept many times, whilst writing this book. She has had to dig back into memories which she'd blocked off, because they hurt too much. Only the extraordinarily powerful passion she felt enabled her to make the cataclysmic decision to leave her child, and Ray sometimes felt quite over-awed at the depth of her sacrifice. 'When we fell in love,' he said to me once, 'we kept saying this is causing too much hurt and pain to too many people, let's stop now but it was unstoppable.'

Together they affected so many lives, not only through Ray's broadcasts but through the palpable strength of their love. It initially caused a lot of heartache but ultimately it enriched everybody around them. David and his wife Julie, who looks uncannily like Alma, both acknowledge that. Ray and Alma's love knew nothing of dominance, or personal ego. The only thing that mattered to either of them was what was better for the other, and it was this passionate selflessness that sustained them through Ray's illness. They were both more concerned for the other than for themselves. 'Do we still laugh?' Alma said in answer to a question only four months before her husband died. 'Oh crumbs yes. I'll come out with some Northern phrase and Ray will fall on the floor laughing. He'll say, "Honestly Alma, you are a case".'

Personally, I feel enormously lucky to have known them because they taught me a lot about both living to one's full capacity and dying without being afraid. Alma was helped by supportive friends, particularly Salvation Army Commissioner Harry Read who was a constant source of strength with his wisdom, unflinching faith, comforting presence and his ability to make sense of what seems inexplicable.

After the funeral he sent a letter to me which I treasure. Towards the end he wrote, 'In spite of what people imagine, funerals do tend to be different, one from the other. Always there is sadness, but with some, there is great despair and the evidence of an almost unhealable wound. Sometimes there is a matter of factness which is disturbing. But on Wednesday, though there was sadness and more than the usual number of brave smiles, there were moments of greatness, when we were conscious of that other world, the existence of which many ignore, but which alone gives meaning to our lives.'

He was the one who helped take away the fear from Ray and also the corrosive bitterness, which a man of forty-five is tortured by when he's told that he will be dead within two years. Fundamentally, however, with Harry Read's help, Alma worked out her own philosophy which was based on what was best for Ray, and to that end she would do literally anything. There were tears in their Blackheath cottage with views over the heath but finally there was also a remarkable kind of peace.

Their relationship had always been an amalgam of tears and laughter since they'd both made tremendous sacrifices to be together. So many people look back with regret or sadness because they didn't value the happy times but this is certainly not true of Alma today. 'This is just a little hiccup for us,' she said five months before Ray died, 'but if it all ends tomorrow we've had a super life.' Ray and Alma fulfilled all their dreams and today she is not tortured with endless 'If onlys . . .' They were married for nearly twenty years and her main feeling, apart from grief, is thankfulness that she was lucky enough to be loved by Ray and to have had so many years of happiness and laughter with him, in their various homes in his beloved Blackheath.

Other young men dream of Paris and New York. But in his mother's little terraced house in the area of Liverpool known as Waterloo, Ray dreamed of the trees, pubs, and open spaces of Blackheath. He used to read Michael Frayn in the old *Manchester Guardian* extolling the eccentric charms of this London village and Ray and Alma's earliest days of unmarried passion, were in a furnished Blackheath studio flat. They toasted their first rented home in a bottle of Lutomer Riesling and anecdotes about Reg, the Blackheath fishmonger, were to be a regular occurrence on the Ray Moore show. 'Have this on me,' Reg the fish said to Alma recently after she'd chosen some giant prawns and smoked salmon. When she demurred he said, 'Well I didn't do anything for the funeral and I know Ray's up there saying, "Reg, you didn't send me any bloody flowers did you?"' 'This calls for a bottle of wine,' said Alma meaning that she would open an accompanying bottle when she got home. 'Hang on a minute,' said Reg the fish in alarm, 'I'm not treating you to the wine as well.'

Ray has left a wonderful legacy of laughter to his friends. And it's not only remembered laughter, but new laughter which always erupts whenever any of his mates gather together. There can be few funerals where one of the mourners would complain as comedian Barry Cryer did on the day Ray was buried, 'Well I didn't think there were enough jokes.' There are indeed few funerals where the wine and the wit flow non stop. So did the anecdotes about Ray, including the account of the letter he sent to his friend, music publisher Tony Peters. It was written to explain why he wouldn't be able to travel north to run in the last Children in Need appeal jog, which Greater Manchester Radio were organising. 'These ingrowing toe nails are a terrible problem,' he wrote in jest, when in truth his body was emaciated, the hole in his throat was growing daily and death was only weeks away.

Today, Alma lives alone, in the enchantingly pretty cottage which they bought four years ago. It has wonderful views in front over the heath and a terrace at the back, where the sun always seems to shine. Her much loved plants are thriving, and, though Alma is bereft, so ultimately will she. She's a fighter, a survivor, a proud Lancastrian who still looks around her elegant sitting room and thinks, 'Not bad for a girl who grew up in a two-up two-down in Salford.' Losing somebody you loved beyond life itself can destroy you but Alma isn't a quitter. She's not hiding away from the world. She cries behind locked doors and then puts on the glitz and goes out to face the world. She never let Ray down when he was alive and she's damned sure she's not going to do so now.

The title of this book, *Tomorrow – Who Knows?* is the refrain from a song that Alma composed many years ago. She wrote it on the train travelling from London to Manchester, when she was making her monthly trek back north, to see her young son David. She didn't know then that tomorrow held a brilliant career for Ray, in which she would be totally involved, that her yearning to retain David's love and respect would be granted. She didn't know that she and Ray would have a marriage that utterly fulfilled them both, that the critics who said, 'He's far too young for you, he'll leave you one day for somebody else,' would be utterly confounded. In fact, taking things all round, Tomorrow for quite a long time proved to be pretty marvellous.

This book is fundamentally a love story about two working-class Northerners brought up in the backstreets of Liverpool and Salford. They came to London with nothing but a shared suitcase, their charm, their talent, their love for each other and they conquered the city.

Part one

ALMA'S STORY

[1]

After Ray died in January 1989, I kept thinking about the Christmas we'd just shared and how against all the odds we'd been so happy. We'd had the most wonderful Christmas on our own, the best we'd ever had.

Everybody was worried about us beforehand. We had so many invitations from friends. My son David and his wife Julie wanted us to spend Christmas with them in Salford. It would have been lovely, but we realised there would be a lot of other family there, and it would have been too much for Ray. Everybody was concerned that we'd be on our own. They were all very caring and worried about us.

In the end, I left the decision to Ray. I said, 'What do you want to do, love?' and he said, 'I'd like Christmas to be just the two of us', which is exactly what I wanted as well. At first I thought, 'I'll not do all the Christmas trimmings this year, what's the point?' Then I thought, 'Yes I certainly will'. We had a Christmas tree in the hall, all the cards up. On Christmas morning I laid the table with lovely flowers, red napkins, red candles. We both got dressed up.

I'd given Ray two smart buttoned-up sweaters for Christmas which he loved and he wore one of them, which was sky blue. He made the stuffing, carved the turkey, we opened a very good bottle of claret. It was almost like going on a date together for the first time. Ray was so poorly but he'd gone out and bought me a beautiful little Victorian gold brooch, with diamonds and rubies, from the jeweller in Blackheath. We couldn't get any closer, because we were always close, but on Christmas Day we sat together in the sitting room, not saying anything and the silence was very rich. I loved him so much, he loved me. In his Christmas card he wrote, 'Darling Alma, I would not be here today without all your love and strength. Now, more than ever, I love you with all my heart'.

It was his birthday on January 2nd and some very dear friends, Jim and Freda Powell, who used to be our neighbours before we moved, asked us if we'd like to spend the day with them.

It was only a week before he died, but Ray got up in the morning, had a bath, got dressed, put on all his best gear and dabbed on lots of Cacharel. I said, 'We can still say "no" if you want to,' but he said, 'I'd like to go', and Jim came round to collect us about one o'clock. When we got there, they had their granddaughters staying with them. As we walked into the sitting room these two little girls in their best frocks sang 'Happy Birthday, dear Ray' and I think we all felt a bit choked.

Ray sat in the corner of the sofa and he just nestled there, looking so comfortable, surrounded with lots of cushions. Jim asked him what he'd like to drink and Ray said, 'A little red wine please,' which Jim knew of course. It took Ray a great effort to speak by this time. All the muscles around his jaw were affected, and he couldn't move his mouth or his tongue. When people saw the dressing they thought he just had an external wound, but the cancer was all inside his mouth as well. Freda said, 'Ray just tell us when you've had enough and Jim will run you home' but he said, 'I'm enjoying myself'.

We all sat there for about four hours, drinking wine, remembering and laughing about the old days. When Ray became ill Jim had been so upset he just hadn't been able to come and see him and I'm so thankful that he was able to resolve his fear before it was too late. Ray didn't talk much, it was too difficult for him by this time, but he was listening and smiling. We'd no idea that it was the last day he'd ever go out in his life. We were talking about how poor we were in the early days. Ray liked the good things, but we were just as happy when we first came to London, when we had nothing. We always said we could cope with anything as long as we had each other.

Right until ten days before he died, Ray was still walking into the village each morning. When he first got the cancer in his mouth, I knew the hole would begin to bleed and ooze particularly in the night. I thought, 'Right, what have I got to do to help Ray?' I knew how terrified he was of leaving any stains in the bed. He was such a meticulous man, it was his one dread. It harked back to his incontinence as a child, when his mother used to get so annoyed with him. He had an absolute phobia about it. Up to this moment, I'd never had a washing machine in my life. I did all the small things by hand and the bigger linen went to the laundry.

After Ray became ill, some days I was washing till midday. Ray said, 'I'm not having that!' and he went out and bought a washing machine. He used to get up every morning about six and bring me a cup of tea. Then he'd take all the loose linen off the bed and put it in the washing machine. I used to get very soft towels and I cut up soft, white sheets, to put them all round the pillow and on top of the bed. Ray had an extra towel as well and I'd put waterproofs inside the pillow case.

He wasn't a bit domesticated or mechanically minded but he made me tell him exactly how to work the washing machine and he wrote it all down. Just recently, I found the list of instructions in his handwriting.

When he'd put all the linen into the machine, he'd sit in the kitchen window looking out over the garden and practising his meditation. His faith healer, who is a lady called Betty Shine, had taught him how to do it. The principle is that you visualise your illness in front of you. You imagine the good cells knocking out the bad cells, a bit like a battle. The hope is that if you can do that, your immune system will start working again. Betty concentrates on mind healing, which is basically using your own mind energy to control the illness and the pain. It helped both of us to cope with Ray's illness.

More and more, doctors believe that cancer is to do with stress and that often it happens to people who can't express anger. Ray certainly wasn't a person ever to show anger, he'd never even use the slightest swear word. If anything went wrong, I'd stamp about and shout, 'Oh honestly, bloody hell'. But Ray used to say, 'I don't really like you swearing Alma'. I could get rid of my annoyance by yelling and banging about. Unfortunately, with people like Ray, all the stress goes inside and rots them from within. I used to admire Ray's calmness but now I think the freer you are, the safer it is. Just being able to slam a door when you're angry is a good thing. And he could always hide his feelings when it came to work. When his father died and Ray had to go on air he still did a very good show even though he felt as if he was dying inside.

He could show emotion in a romantic way. He'd sit with the tears pouring down his face when we were listening to romantic music, but he couldn't show anger, however justified it might have been. The romance stayed with us all our lives, he was just so caring and a real softie. A lot of people in the business used to say to him, 'Ray you've got to be harder, got to be pushy,' but it wasn't his nature. He said to me once, 'Why do I have to change? I'm doing a job I love and I haven't got it by being pushy'. He was probably right, because he wouldn't have lived easily if he'd done anything he didn't really approve of.

Going out and acting the star wasn't his way and Ray didn't like to feel too safe. That's why he was happy as a freelance rather than being on the staff of the BBC. He said that when broadcasters feel safe and cosy, they lose their cutting edge. He went freelance in 1973 and he always felt it kept him on his toes, kept him sharp and all his wits about him. I think in the end though, he fell foul of trying to do too much, he was really shattered. I'd look at his diary and think, 'This is ridiculous'.

After he'd had his morning tea, Ray would have his bath whilst I'd be in the bedroom preparing his dressings. I liked to have everything ready in neat little piles and then I could be really efficient. Because of the position of the cancer, it was difficult to get at, so Ray would lie across the bottom of the bed, then I could sit on the side next to him. We got it all worked out. I had to clean the wound and Ray always said, 'Nobody does it like you Alma'. I used to try and make the dressing into a really neat shape so that he felt good. I'd do it so he felt safe. The district nurses were so nice, they were real pets. The senior nurse said, 'I want to come and watch how you do it Alma, because we know how vital it is to Ray, to feel secure'. As the wound got worse it had to be dressed three times a day but it wasn't a chore. I just used to think how wonderful it was that I could still do it, that it was still just Ray and I, coping on our own.

I looked on it as a privilege to look after him. We were just totally together in our little cottage and the world was outside. We'd put Radio 3 on very quietly and he'd lie there until I'd finished fastening all the dressings. He would never look at the wound. He thought of it as something outside him, that had nothing to do with Ray. Once by accident, he got just a glimpse of it in the bathroom mirror and he was absolutely appalled. He said, 'Alma I don't know how you can bear to look at this three times a day'. I said, 'Well you'd do the same for me,' and he said 'Oh, Alma I couldn't'. He was always saying, 'It's nothing to do with me this cancer, it's merely something that's attached itself to me'. He also said that if I hadn't been there, he'd just have crawled away and licked his wounds like a dog. Whenever he'd been ill before, he'd say, 'Just leave me alone, I'll be all right'. He always had this great conviction that the body was stronger than you thought and that it can cast off any illness.

In the beginning, I didn't realise how the cancer would progress, though one specialist had told us that it would turn into a gaping hole. In those last days, it had just got to his lower lip and that was the only time I was frightened of doing the dressing. I thought, 'What if it goes on spreading, what's going to happen to his bottom lip?' But I was able to do it right until the end, even the night before he died I couldn't really see the jawbone any more, whether or not there was any, I don't know. I thought, 'Dear God, you can't let him go on disappearing before my eyes'. This is what does happen to some people. They have to wear a mask in the end. But the good God was merciful, he decided the suffering should stop.

When Ray first stopped broadcasting after the cancer was diagnosed, he just used to mooch about in the day, go to the pub and have too much beer, then he'd sleep in the afternoon. Whenever anything had been troubling us, all our lives, we'd always talked about it. Usually it would be Ray who would say, 'Alma we have to have a little talk,' but this time it was me, because at that period in our lives, I was the stronger. I said, 'Ray, you've got to have a discipline in your day'. He'd been asked to write a book and I said, 'You want to do this book and you've got to work at it. Every morning, once we've done the dressings you must go into your study and start to write.' This is what he did, and he found he loved writing. He'd always wanted to, but previously there had never been enough time. In the end he was compelled by necessity and not by choice. When he was writing his first book he'd read things out to me and I'd say, 'Ray I think this is smashing'. He'd laugh and say, 'Well you would, wouldn't you?'

Once he started writing, he felt he had a plan for the day, there was a pattern to his life. He needed this because he'd always been such a worker. Ray was a funny mixture. Nobody enjoyed luxury more, but he had such a puritanical streak. He could never have been happy unless he felt he was achieving something. He'd write all morning, and then we'd walk across to our local pub, the Railway Tavern, which he used to call the Shopper's Rest. We'd have a drink, say 'Hello' to a few friends and then walk home. Towards the end the walk got slower and slower. I'd link arms with him because he needed the support, just to steady him.

He was writing his second book until about two weeks before he died. He'd be so pleased if he knew that I'd end up writing part of it as well, but then I'm sure he does know. I feel such a strong sense of him being around me, particularly in our cottage. People have said, 'How can you bear to stay there?' but it's the place where I feel least alone.

Ray would only ever write in the mornings. At lunchtime, we'd just have some soup and then he'd lie down and have a sleep, but he hated sleeping when the sun was shining. He wanted to be out there, enjoying it. Afterwards, I'd go out for a jog so I could be on my own for a bit, regain my strength. I used to pray quite a lot when I was jogging but I was always very wary that I shouldn't ask for too much. I used to pray more than Ray but I never actually said, 'Please God, make Ray better'. I only ever asked, 'Please God, give both Ray and me the strength to cope with whatever comes along'. Now, I still pray for strength to cope and I also pray that perhaps I can help other people. I feel whatever I've been given, both in experience and in money, I must use. I feel I've been left like this because there is something waiting for me to do. I still cry a lot but it's never when you think you're going to. It's not when you're feeling terribly low but at a time when just for the moment you're feeling all right and then the grief just totally overwhelms you without any warning.

Before he died, Ray kept saying, 'Alma, whatever happens, when I'm dead, you mustn't waste the rest of your life'. I used to worry about how I'd cope with the press when he died and he said, 'Alma you've got to do it your way, but don't take any nonsense from any of the family'.

He surprised me with what he was able to cope with. The pain must have been appalling though he never said so. The tears would well up in his eyes. He always insisted on getting dressed and going out. It would have been so easy just to stay at home but he said, 'I'm not letting you down, I'm not hiding, I'm not a criminal'. One of the doctors at the hospital said to him once, 'Do you drink?' and Ray said, 'If you had this, wouldn't you drink?' He didn't like to be totally without pain. If he wasn't in pain, he felt the painkillers he was taking were too strong. He wouldn't have them at all in the beginning and then only the very weakest. One of the nurses said, 'Ray we know why you're getting the pain. We can't do anything about the cancer. But we can do something about that pain'.

That last year, the whole pattern of our day was geared to Ray. He'd look through the window and see me setting off on my jog and then he'd watch me coming back across the heath. In the early evening he'd say, 'I think it's time for a little drink,' and he'd have a glass of red wine and pour me out a vodka and tonic. I'd always begin to speak and he'd interrupt and say, 'Yes I know, you just want a weak one'. I felt a great emotional thankfulness inside that we were looking after ourselves and I know it helped Ray. He didn't want people coming in and out.

He was having vitamins crushed, high doses of vitamin C, all the things we knew would help him cope and they did. Even when he was very ill he was still doing the washing up after supper. He used to say, 'I can still wash up'. I'd go downstairs to the sitting room and he'd make the coffee and bring it down. I had decaffeinated and every night he'd say, 'I've got two cups on this tray, why is it always yours that spills?'. We'd watch the early news programme on Channel 4 and then I'd go and prepare his evening dressing. When I'd finished, I'd shout 'Ready for you'. It began to take longer and longer as the hole got bigger but doing it was always a precious time together. I kept thanking God I had the strength to do it. He used to say, 'I don't need to have a painting of myself in the attic like Dorian Gray because I'm slowly becoming that painting'. He'd make jokes about his speech when friends came round but really it upset him terribly. The only way he could cope with his grief was to joke about it. His voice had been so superb but gradually he could scarcely move his lips or his tongue.

After we'd done the dressing, he'd have another glass of red wine and then go to bed. The extraordinary thing was that he slept very well and he certainly wasn't on very large doses of painkillers. I never felt exhausted, I was leading a very healthy life. I was jogging everyday and eating well. I was insistent on lots of fresh vegetables, lots of fruit and fish for Ray. I had the same and I liquidised everything for him. Really it was a very healthy time for me which was good, because I needed to keep strong. Afterwards, all the nurses and doctors said it was unbelievable that Ray didn't take to his bed till the last seven days and I'm sure it was because of the way we lived.

In early January, our lovely GP Desmond popped in as he often did. He said, 'You look a bit pale Ray, you might be anaemic. I'll just do a blood test'. Ray said, 'No wonder I'm anaemic, I'm losing all this blood and now you're taking even more.' Even then, right at the end of his life, he was still joking. Desmond came back with the result next day and he said, 'It's fine. All it proved is that there's not as much red wine in your blood as usual!' Ray loved wine and he loved friends coming round for a drink. It was a pleasure always to watch him going round with a bottle. He'd never let anybody be standing with a glass half full, it had to be full. Because he knew I hated cooking, we never gave dinner parties but we'd have a houseful over for drinks and I'd just do lots of cocktail snacks.

Then, as we got more money, we'd book a little room in a restaurant and invite a few friends to have dinner with us. We'd start with champagne and we'd choose the menu in advance. We used to go to The Kaya, which is a little Korean restaurant in Soho, and Ray adored it. The food is very delicate and spiced with lots of different little dishes. We had a wonderful evening there once with Terry and Helen Wogan, Phil Sellers who was financial director at British Rail, Adrian John and his wife Joy, David and Julie and a few other friends.

We also used to give breakfasts at the St George's Hotel, which is just opposite Broadcasting House, after Ray had done his early morning show. We'd start off with champagne because Ray would come off the air very high, the adrenalin was flowing and it would be like lunch-time for him. We'd suddenly give a breakfast party for no reason at all, perhaps life was just seeming a bit dull at the time. Ray was a wonderful host, he could talk on almost any subject, and he had this amazing memory. He could remember tiny little incidents from his childhood, and if he read anything, it was all filed away in his brain. He'd hear odd phrases when we were out and he'd write them on the back of his cigarette packet.

When I was a kid, I used to cycle to a place near Salford called Boggart Hole Clough. In those days we thought it was the real country and Ray loved this name. He used to make things up about it when he was doing the programme. He just appealed to so many people. He got letters from little old ladies, lawyers, academics, real high fliers and they were all totally in rapport with him. He always said that they could pick out of the programme what they chose.

It was a great pleasure to nurse him in that last year and he never complained. Even when he was in pain, his face would just pucker up. He was always apologetic and he was so thin, poor little lamb, you just wanted to pick him up and hug him. Ray refused to have any operation or radiotherapy and so many people I respect, including our own GP, say he was right. I think doctors have got to reconsider the whole thing concerning cancer of the mouth because it's such a drastic operation. It doesn't seem to do any good, only cause suffering and distress. Most of Ray's tongue would have gone and his jawbone; there would have been terrible pain from skin and bone grafts. Because he didn't have the operation Ray had another six months of broadcasting, we enjoyed two lovely holidays and at the end the whole family were able to cherish and care for him at home.

On January 3rd he got dressed but he said, 'I don't feel like going out today.' The next day he got up, did all his usual things. He brought me tea in bed, did his meditation. I was just getting out of bed when he came in the bedroom and he said, 'I'm going to go back to bed,' which was unheard of. He didn't want anything to eat and he seemed to be getting weaker and weaker. The Macmillan nurse came round and she said, 'You do realise he's in a phase don't you?', and I knew she meant it could be the death phase. Possibly because we'd had all those months to prepare for it this wasn't a great shock. Ray had no fear by this time, there was a certain acceptance. We'd had so much time to say everything we wanted to say to each other, to talk of our love and we also talked about death. So many people can't say the word and it becomes a terrible huge barrier between you.

Once you've said it, then it's just another word. How you cope with the death of somebody you love very much does depend on the person who has died. If he leaves you with the legacy of feeling that life is not over then that is a tremendous strength.

Later that day, Desmond, our local GP, came round and he was very caring as he always has been. His father Brian used to be our GP and he took over from him. It's one of those lovely, totally committed family practices that you think don't exist any more. Once when Ray had 'flu, Brian came round with a bottle of whisky. He said, 'I've brought you some really good medicine'.

This time Desmond said, 'Let's just have a little chat Alma'. He said, 'Obviously you realise that Ray is getting much worse'. I said, 'Yes'. He said, 'I don't see how you can cope on your own. Would you like me to ring the local hospice and let them know that we might need a bed?' I said, 'Perhaps it would be a good idea.' And then in the afternoon, the Macmillan lady doctor came round and Ray loved her. She was very special and supportive to both of us. She talked to Ray as though he were a human being which wasn't always true of the consultants. She totally understood his fear and she gave us all the information in a calm, gentle way. When she first saw Ray she said, 'I'd like to examine the tumour, I do need to see what's going on behind the dressing'. Ray was happy about that because at University College Hospital some doctors treated him without ever looking at the tumour.

This particular morning she sat on the bed and chatted to him. She said, 'How do you feel about going to the hospice, Ray?' He said, 'If that's the best thing'. She then asked him, 'Ray would you really like to stay at home?' and he said, 'If it's possible'. She replied, 'I think it's quite possible. Alma has proved she's absolutely capable. If she gets some help from the family and feels she can cope, then we'll work on those lines'.

She came into the kitchen and she asked me if there was

anybody in the family who could help. I said, 'I'm sure Ray's mother and his sister Jan will come.' I rang up his Mum and I said, 'Ray's really taken a turn for the worse'. Straight away she said, 'I'll come and help and I'm sure Jan will come as well'. She phoned Jan at the NatWest Bank in Crosby village, near Liverpool, where she works and rang me back. She said they were coming and I felt quite relieved. I thought, 'Great. I must tell Ray'.

I ran into the bedroom and he was sitting on the edge of the bed. I said, 'Ray love, what are you doing?' He said, 'I've got to get dressed.' I said, 'It's all right love, there's nothing to worry about. You've no dates, no appointments, nobody's coming, get back into bed.' I then said, 'I must tell you what I've done, I've asked Mum and Jan to come,' and he was upset. He said, 'What have you asked them for?' He didn't want anyone else near him, he only wanted me. I said, 'I know you're angry, but try and look at it as though they're doing me a favour. Mum can look after the food, Jan will take care of the phone and I can look after you. It really would be a great help to me'.

He said 'All right' but I did understand how he felt. He loved his mother dearly. He admired her for what she'd achieved, how she'd worked, kept the family together. But he didn't want her to see him in that state. He was the eldest son, the one going back home from London, buying the champagne and taking them all out. When his father left them for five years, because of his drinking problem, Ray felt he had to be the big boy, look after the other kids. Ray had such a sense of responsibility towards the family. He always wanted to be the one caring for them. His mother was terrified of any of them turning to drink. She used religion to try and keep them off the drink. Every Sunday they had to go to church three times but it didn't work. Both Ray and his brother Don drank a lot.

By this time I had to lean very close to him to know what he was saying. I'd put my ear to his lips and he couldn't talk a lot but he used to squeeze my hand. He'd try and nod his head. I think that by this time, whatever secondary cancers he had were affecting him. The doctors didn't know where they were. Ray wasn't X-rayed, he didn't have any scans because he didn't want to and he was right. What would it have proved? Only that he had another cancer. I think a lot of people condemned us because we didn't always take the doctor's advice, but we didn't make any decision lightly. We read everything we could possibly read on the subject, we did endless research. There was little we didn't know about cancer of the mouth in the end.

Early that evening, Jan and Ray's Mum arrived, Mum with her hat on. I explained the situation. I didn't go out of the house again till after Ray died. Mum brewed up, made the meals, Jan took over the phone and it worked very well. David and Julie came on the Saturday which was January 7th and that was a great comfort. I'd never really been involved with a person who was dying before and I'd thought I was going to be afraid. It's a very dreadful experience to go through, but there was a lot about it that was beautiful. It sounds a funny word to use but that's how it was. Everything at the end was very calm.

I do believe so many people praying for him, beaming their love on him, meant that a miracle did occur. He died in peace, without pain, without anything awful happening and that was the miracle we were given.

The last couple of days he couldn't speak, we didn't think he could see. His Mum and Jan were there and we'd take it in turns to hold his hand, reassure him that he was in his own bed, in his own house, overlooking the heath that he loved. That last week of his life he looked so frail, I didn't want anybody to see him, and then I thought, 'Hang on Alma, how dare you? Ray may well be lying there wondering why no friends are coming to see him'.

I said, 'Right, I know exactly what I'm going to do'. I rang up Adrian John and his wife and Colin Berry and his wife because we've all been such good friends. I said, 'I'd like you to come and say goodbye to Ray,' and they cried. They said, 'We wanted to but we didn't like to ask'. They came over and I just took them in two at a time and I said, 'Two lovely friends are here to see you Ray'.

Afterwards we opened a bottle of champagne and said, 'Cheers Ray, we love you dearly,' and we had a laugh, recalling many hilarious escapades from the past. Ray's Mum and his sister Jan haven't lived the life we lived and I was a bit worried about them. I thought they might not understand. Then I thought, 'Hang on Alma, this is your house, your husband. You must do what you think is right,' and Mum and Jan were great. They were joining in and laughing. I seemed to be guided in everything I decided, but it was nothing I could have planned in advance. I told Harry Read, Ray's friend from the Salvation Army, what I'd done and he said, 'You were quite right. Although Ray isn't speaking now, he's still aware of our presence. He needs to see friends that he's known and loved and had fun with.'

During those last few days I didn't want people creeping about, whispering, talking in hushed voices. I wanted everything to be just as it always was for Ray, not some awful house of doom and gloom. I used to be in the bedroom chattering away to him. I'd say, 'I'm putting my face on now Ray'. I just kept him filled in with what was happening each day and reassuring him about what a wonderful life I'd had with him. I kept telling him, 'I'm so pleased I met you Ray, aren't I lucky?' I said, 'Do you remember how we went on Colin and Sandra's honeymoon with them? And how you broke your foot and Terry Wogan used to make all those jokes about it on his morning programme?' We always used to laugh about Terry saying on air, 'Can

[43]

you believe it? Ray Moore broke his foot on Colin Berry's honeymoon.' I talked about Harry Read and about David and Julie and baby Paul. I wanted Ray to feel natural, as though things in the house were as they always had been. I kept reassuring him that he was in his own bedroom. I'd look out of the window and say, 'Just look at that traffic jam on Shooters Hill', which there was every morning. I saw some children out on the heath with kites and I talked about the kite he'd bought for Paul. I didn't see why near the end of his life we should all be whispering. Ray would have absolutely hated that. Rightly or wrongly I did what I thought was best and just chattered away to him.

Ray adored a drink, he was always saying, 'Let's open a bottle'. Towards the end, I did think of rubbing some wine on his lips but I just smoothed on some glycerine and lemon and I bet he thought 'Ugh'. He loved Cacharel and I sprayed it around his pillow. I made him absolutely comfortable. You always imagine death is going to be horrible, but I was damned determined he had to have dignity all the time because it would have mattered a lot to him.

On Wednesday January 11th, it was clear he was just going gently. Mum and his brother Don were in with him but I didn't leave anybody with him for too long. I liked to be there, because I could always sense if Ray was getting agitated. I could tell if he wanted anything, when other people wouldn't know. Don came into the kitchen and said, 'Mum thinks you'd better come back Alma'. I went and then Mum said, 'We'll leave you with Ray now'. I spoke to him gently but he couldn't reply, there was no squeeze of the hand. I was taking his pulse and it was getting weaker and weaker. I didn't actually say goodbye to him, I don't see it as goodbye. I just told him I loved him very much which I was always telling him all the time. And he was still saying it to me that whole last week until he couldn't speak. I just held

[44]

him till I was sure Ray wasn't there any more and then I tidied the bedclothes and I went into the kitchen. I got another bottle of champagne out of the fridge and we all had a drink. We said, 'Cheers, Ray. You're free now. Go and enjoy it'.

He'd been nursed in his own bed, right until the end with me next to him, everybody he loved was there, we never left him on his own. I just felt so happy that he was rid of that dreadful thing because it was awful. He must have felt 'I've had enough'. During that last year I sustained him and he sustained me. He always said, 'In broadcasting you've got to get the beginning right, the ending right and the middle will look after itself. But the timing is the most important thing'. He certainly got the timing right this time and apart from the hole in my life I felt quite happy.

I hadn't known what I was going to be like when he died. I thought I might fall to pieces. I still might but I'm just thankful that he's free. There was also a sense of great relief that he was out of that shell of a body that was letting him down. He was a very special guy, a lovely, lovely man. It was a great honour to have shared twenty years of his life. Right to the end he knew we were all there, we just surrounded him with our love. Afterwards I kept thinking, 'Hang on, I should be sitting around in widow's weeds with everybody looking after me,' but I didn't feel like that. I felt strong. I felt positive. In the evening we said, 'What would Ray have liked?' We said, 'Fish and chips and champagne,' and that's what we had.

[2]

Ray and I actually grew up only about thirty miles away from each other. He was born in Park House Nursing Home in Liverpool in January 1942 and I was born in Hope Hospital in Salford in January 1933. We were both Capricorn which means that when things were good between us they were brilliant and when they were bad they were terrible.

In the early 1920s, my mother had got married to a merchant seaman and they had two children, a boy and a girl. I don't think he was a very good husband and eventually she split up from him and then she met my father. They lived together for years and didn't get married till I was a teenager. I have a real sister, Audrey, two years older than me, but I haven't seen her for twenty-five years. She had some terrible row with my mother and neither of us ever saw her again. After all the publicity about Ray one of her daughters contacted me. She said she knew of Ray but she hadn't known that her mother's sister was married to him. Audrey is a widow now and I think her daughter feels she's lonely, but I wasn't close to my sister and she has five children and has a life of her own. We used to fight like cat and dog when we were children and then she married a regular soldier and lived in Hong Kong for a while and in Germany.

I didn't know my parents weren't married till I was a teenager. My sister found out and told me and I can remember thinking it was quite exciting and saying, 'Hey, I'm a bastard'. In those days everything was covered up, you didn't talk about things, everybody wanted to be what was called respectable. One of my mother's sisters said to me once, 'Do you know anything about what happened?' and when I said, 'What are you talking about?' she just said, 'Oh never mind, but I do think your mother ought to have told you'. I did quite often wonder who was this girl called Kathleen, who kept coming to visit the house. We were always sent out to play when she arrived, and I thought she was some vague, distant cousin. Of course she was the daughter by my mother's first marriage and my Grandma and two maiden aunts brought her up. I think her father was a bit of a rotter but it was all kept quiet.

My mother is a very strong lady, still living on her own aged ninety-one. My father was a real softie. He had charm but he also had a lot of weaknesses. He signed on for the First World War when he was seventeen by telling the authorities he was eighteen. He ultimately found himself in the fields of France, where he was badly wounded. After the war, when he got home, he didn't have any skills and he used to do casual work on Salford docks. I can remember him going out in the morning and then coming back because the bloke who was choosing that day's team of dockers hadn't picked him.

My mother was a tailoress so she could always get work. There's an area around Manchester called Cheetham Hill, which is a very Jewish area where all the rag trade is based, and my mother used to work there in a little factory. She went out to work all during the depression, because my father couldn't get any jobs on the docks, and he looked after my sister and me. We lived in a little rented, terraced house in Harmsworth Street, Seedley which is an area of Salford. It had no bathroom, the lavatory was in the back yard. There were two bedrooms and a front room where my mother kept all the best furniture. The front door, which was on the street, opened on to a little vestibule. You then had to walk through this wonderful front room, to get to the back. But that was all we ever did, walk through it. It was all highly polished and you weren't allowed to touch anything, it was kept for Best, whatever that might be. You certainly weren't allowed to sit down in it. There was a little strip of special carpet you had to walk on, so you wouldn't damage the floor. We lived in the kitchen where there was an old black-leaded grate. Outside, there was a zinc bath which hung on a nail in the yard and every Friday it would be brought into the kitchen and we'd have a bath.

As a kid it used not to worry me. I thought the way we lived was like everybody else. I then passed the scholarship to go to the High School and got called a snob by the other kids which made me very upset. The feeling was that if you were going to the High School you had ideas above your station and ought to be brought down a few pegs, which says a lot for our street.

Sometimes we'd have parties at home. These were those rare occasions when we were allowed to use the front room. My Auntie Nell would play the piano and my mother would sing because she's a wonderful singer. As a girl she'd wanted to go on the stage. She thought she'd have been another Gracie Fields who was about the same age and came from Rochdale which isn't far away. She used to say to Ray, 'The only reason I didn't go on the stage was because in those days you didn't go against your parents'. Ray of course had gone right against his father's wishes by going into the theatre and then doing radio. He'd say to my mother, 'If you'd wanted to do it badly enough, you'd have found the courage,' but she wouldn't accept that.

She really did have a beautiful contralto voice. She used to sing at the Theatre Royal Cinema in Manchester and the Ambassador in Salford during the silent film era. Violet Carson was playing the piano in cinemas at the same time on the same circuit. My mother would sing emotional songs during any romantic scene. She once sang 'La Marseillaise' in English for *The Four Horsemen of the Apocalypse*. Her uncle was fluent in

French and he translated it for her. She used to sing Tosti's 'Forever' which was very popular and 'Abide with Me'. When the film *Peg of my Heart* was being shown, there was an entire stage set before the film began with covered wagons and everybody dressed as Red Indians. My mother sang 'The Old Folks at Home', then another lady sang 'Love's Old Sweet Song'. A little boy sang 'Oh Susannah' and then the film started. Sometimes they'd have an entire orchestra or an organ accompanying her instead of just a piano. My mother's real name was Mary Pollitt but when she was singing she called herself Mae Pollitt.

I think the reason she could sometimes be very sharp with us kids was because of her frustration and bitterness about not going on with her singing.

I love her because she's my mother, I admire her a lot, I admire her strength, her hard work and because she's a real survivor but she's trodden on a few toes in her life. She's a very intelligent lady, very sociable. Everybody who meets her says what a wonderful old lady she is, she'll crack jokes with you, be cheeky. But there's another side to her, a darker side that she doesn't let anybody see but me. She'll always put a front on for other people, pretend everything is wonderful when it isn't. I'm a bit like that but I'm trying to change. I can't really cope with her, I feel upset every time I leave.

The first year Ray and I were in our little Blackheath house she came for Christmas with David and Julie. I'd spent ages trying to find her a beautiful pair of earrings. On Christmas morning we were all unwrapping our presents, Ray had opened the champagne. My mother took the earrings out, stared at them and all she said was, 'You usually have such good taste, Alma'. The first day the shops were open after Christmas I went back to the shop and brought about fifteen pairs of earrings home for her to choose her own from. I never answer her back and I think that's probably a mistake and really I should have said a long time ago, 'Mum why do you behave like this?' It's as much my fault as hers.

Ken Bruce spent Christmas with us that year as well. He's such a lovely man. He used to be an announcer too, like Ray, and they were so funny together. We'd go out with him and he and Ray would help to get rid of the French wine lake. They'd both get maudlin and keep saying, 'If our broadcasting work ended tomorrow we'd be all right, we could still be announcers'.

During that Christmas period Ken was going through a difficult time. His lovely wife had come to England from Scotland to try and make a go of their marriage but it hadn't worked, so she'd gone back home with the two children. Ray and I related so much to how he must be feeling and Ray rang him up. He said, 'Ken, if at any point over the holiday you'd like a drink and a natter then we're here'. Ken came over on Christmas Day after he'd done his programme at Broadcasting House, and he was wonderful with my mother. He was in the kitchen helping us prepare everything for the Christmas dinner, paper hats, crackers and so forth. We stayed up really late, playing old records. He and Ray were tucking into the vino collapsus, and in the end he wasn't fit to drive, so he kipped down on the floor.

Afterwards he kept saying, 'I can't thank you enough'. I said, 'We should be thanking you, it was lovely and you were marvellous with my mother'.

When I went in for the scholarship I was at Langworthy Road School in Salford, and then when I'd won it I went to Pendleton High, which was known round our way as PHS which stood for Pig's Home for Snobs. There was quite a strong feeling about the place, going there really did separate you from the kids who didn't. But I was thrilled to bits when I got in, it seemed a very important step, people told me it would change my life. The only trouble was the uniform because we couldn't afford a proper one. My whole outfit was cobbled together, I had a second hand hat and my mother made my navy blue gym slip. It was well sewn because she was a tailoress but I knew it wasn't like the kind everybody else had and I didn't want to be different.

My one pride and joy was my scarf. I had a real new school scarf bought in the proper school shop and I used to swing it nonchalantly round my neck. When I got to the High School, I was amazed because the girls there had clean white socks every single day. Until then, I'd always assumed that everybody turned their socks inside out and wore them again a second day. I stayed to lunch and the first dinnertime I saw I had a knife, fork and spoon in front of me. I ate my meat and vegetables and then I got the spoon and scooped up the gravy. We always had to do that at home so as not to waste anything. The girl next to me said, 'You don't behave like that here. That spoon is for your pudding'. I nearly died with shame because I'd done the wrong thing. I picked up the spoon, licked it clean and put it back.

I wasn't a very good learner at school because I was too impatient. All I really cared about was sport and gymnastics. In the end I had to leave when I was fifteen, before School Certificate. I'd had a few bashes on the knee with hockey sticks and my kneecap suddenly started locking. I had to keep moving it around with my hands, till it unlocked. The doctor got me into Hope Hospital in Salford and they found a cyst there which they removed. It really only needed just a little cut but they opened up the whole knee. I had to have fourteen stitches and I've still got the most horrendous scar.

I was very depressed afterwards and the doctor advised me to start cycling a lot to strengthen my leg. I joined the Mercury Road cycling club and it was through the club that I met my first husband, Roy Mather. He belonged to another club but we used to meet at events at Fallowfield cycle track. I'd cycle home with him and two other lads but he lived nearest to my house. He'd ride with me to the corner of my street, after they'd dropped off. Eventually he started asking me out and I really grew to love him. Before he died, Ray kept saying, 'You must marry again Alma,' but I've been in love twice in my life, they were both smashing guys and I don't feel I can ask for too much more.

Cycling was a big thing then in the north, it was in the wonderful days of Reg Harris. We'd all go out and cycle miles. The longest trip I ever did in one day was cycling from Salford to Chester. We were heading for Llangollen but we never made it. We had great fun, there was no nastiness in the sport, never any trouble. We went all over the place, we went out on Sunday – hail, rain or shine. The big thing on Sundays was the twenty-five-mile road races along the East Lancs road. You'd probably start around five in the morning and a lot of the houses on the route used to do bed and breakfast for about ten bob.

While I was in hospital, the girls in my year were taking the School Certificate so I missed all that. A lot of people, I suppose, would have gone back and done it the following year but I really didn't want to. I searched the *Manchester Evening News* and I noticed in bold, black print the letters BBC. They were advertising for an office junior, so I wrote off for a form and filled it in. It was a job that meant delivering the post to all the different departments. There were a lot of stairs and they were worried about my knee but I said, 'Oh I'm fine. I'm cycling now'.

I got the job and I thought it was terribly exciting, working for the BBC which was right in the centre of Piccadilly in Manchester in those days. My sister and I had been brought up on 'Children's Hour' on the wireless and the broadcasters on the programme were called Aunties and Uncles. I'd go into the canteen, there would be all the Aunties and Uncles and I'd see Judith and Sandra Chalmers who were child actresses and I'd often see Geoffrey and Peter Wheeler in short pants! It was all terribly formal at the BBC in those days. The Controller of North Region and the Assistant Head of Programmes had offices on the top floor. We were told that if ever we bumped into them when we were delivering the post we had to say 'Good morning, Sir'.

The messenger girls still wore ankle socks and we'd dab on a little powder and lipstick but that was all. It was just the time when sweat shirts were all the rage and my friend and I decided to get one each and we thought we looked terrific. A bit of me was very confident and I tried not to show the other bit that wasn't. But once I got settled in at the BBC, it became like home. I was getting paid £2 a week and I loved it. They were golden years, that whole period was a wonderful time. The wireless was so vital to people's lives, I was very proud to work there. I used to love going into the building and saying, when people outside asked me what I did, 'Oh I work at the BBC. I am the pips for the Greenwich time signal!'

If you didn't get another job when you stopped being a junior at eighteen you had to leave but I managed to get a post as a filing clerk and I loved that as well. I used to file all the contracts and reading all the famous names who were broadcasting then was quite thrilling. It's even possible that I may have filed Ray's audition letter to 'Children's Hour'. He passed the audition but they never called him.

Sometimes we were allowed to sit in on recordings. When the Northern Variety Orchestra, under their conductor Ray Martin, were doing a programme we'd go in and sit on the little balcony in Studio One and we thought it was magical. Jimmy

Young used to record sessions with them. In the canteen, the lady manageress really looked after us kids. If there was anything left over we'd always get seconds. By this time, my mother had become head waitress at the Grand Hotel in Manchester which Geoffrey Wheeler's father ran. She loved it but it was hard work, grotty hours. She'd often be there late at nights when they had banquets. I didn't like it too much because she started doing it while I was still at Pendleton High and I can remember going back to the house from school and nobody was ever in.

We all had to help out at home and one of my jobs every Saturday was to sweep the front street and stone steps. I then had to clean them with white stone and the steps to the outside toilet had to be stoned as well. Recently I went back home to see my mother who still lives in the same street and it was just a mess of toffee papers, chip papers, plastic cartons. When I was a kid, times were hard, there was hardly any money, no bathroom, no electricity but that street was immaculate. Everybody swept their front, every step was dazzling white. My mother can't do it herself now, the home help certainly won't do it, but in the old days if there was any old lady living alone, the neighbours would clean the steps for her. I said, 'I'll do it for you Mum,' but she said, 'Oh just leave it. It will be as bad again tomorrow'.

Last time I was there, all the young mums were sitting out on the front doorsteps with their children and the street was filthy. I can't understand that mentality, I'd just have to sweep it. We've become a throw-away country but when I was a kid nobody dropped so much as an apple core. Now they've all got bathrooms, there are cars parked outside nearly every house but the whole place looks a mess. My mother doesn't get out except on Sundays, when all the old people are collected and taken to the local Civic Hall. They are given lunch and the kids who wait on them are first-time offenders. She loves going but I do feel awful when I think apart from that she's sitting inside the house every day. When Ray died she was very low and if I'd let her she'd have sapped me totally. I was a bit short with her I know, but I had to be self protective, it was the only way I could cope.

I started really going out with Roy Mather when I was eighteen, we got engaged at nineteen and married when I was twenty-four. We were having too much of a good time, neither of us wanted to settle down. We also wanted to save enough money to put down a deposit on a house first. Our courting was all very chaste, I was a virgin when I got married. If you were a decent sort of girl in those days then that's how it was. My mother never told me anything about sex, it was just one of those things that you did when you got married. I think it's talked about too much now. Probably some families were too strict in the old days, and messed up their daughters' lives, but most of us were all right. We just went in for what we called heavy petting before we got married. That's one of the things that frightens me about another relationship. I think, perhaps wrongly, that the first thing any man would want to do would be to jump into bed and I couldn't cope with that.

Roy and I got married in September 1956. We had a white wedding, two of my pals from the BBC, Kathy Taylor and Pat Thorpe, were bridesmaids. We had a buffet reception at Binns Café in Eccles Old Road in Salford, and then we drove off in our little old Morris. We spent the first night of our honeymoon in Knutsford before we went driving round Wales. It was exciting but I found that first night very difficult and so did Roy. I'm still very fond of Roy though I'm aware that we've both changed. I have happy memories of the times when we were young together. I've often thought I'd love to spend an evening with him, just to have a natter about the old days now the bitterness has gone.

When Ray and I fell in love and knew that it was absolutely right to be together, I used to pray for Roy to find somebody else and be as happy as Ray and I were. He did marry again, a girl who was much younger and they've got two smashing daughters. His wife can cook, makes jam, bakes wonderful cakes, she does all the things I was no good at. Perhaps that's what he wanted.

Roy was a joiner and carpenter and when we were together his big plan was to save up enough money to buy a piece of land and build his own house. And after I left him this is exactly what he did.

About six months after we got back from our honeymoon I found out I was pregnant. I wasn't pleased at first, it was a bit of a blow. I said to everybody, 'I can't be pregnant. We are saving up for a deposit on a house'. But once I'd got used to the idea I've never felt so well as I did in the next few months. I carried on cycling.

When David was born in December 1957, he was a wonderful bouncing baby. He weighed nine pounds and I had him in Urmston Cottage Hospital. I really loved being there, I did all my exercises and even though he was such a whopper I didn't have to have any stitches. In those days you used to stay in hospital for a fortnight but they let me go home a bit early in time for Christmas Day.

I can remember getting home with this baby wondering what had hit me. I have this vivid recollection of standing at the sink washing nappies with the tears pouring down my face. By this time we'd bought a modern semi in Salford. It needed a lot doing to it which was ideal with Roy being a joiner. David was such a bonny baby with very blond straight hair. I used to put him out in the garden in his pram, even if it was snowing or there was a thunderstorm. In those days you had a big proper pram with a canopy and I'd tuck a hot water bottle in with him. I asked him the other day if he remembered those days when I used to shove him out in his pram, even if it was pouring down with rain. I was breast-feeding him and I had masses of milk. I was on maternity leave and I went back to work when he was two months old.

My mother was working at Boots by this time and she said she'd give up her job and look after David for us in the day. She really did help us out of a hole because I didn't want to give up work, as we needed the money. When I look at David's wife Julie with baby Paul now I think, 'I shouldn't have gone back so soon,' but I don't really think I was cut out to be a mother.

Two or three years before I met Ray, gradually things got difficult between Roy and me. I wasn't happy with my life and I became very sad because I knew Roy loved me, but we couldn't talk about things. Every morning my mother would collect David and in the afternoon she'd bring him back and wait till we got home. I missed out on a lot of David's childhood but I'm lucky in that I'm gaining from being so close to him today. My mother feels that she totally brought him up. She was very angry on the phone one day. She said, 'David never comes to see me. And after all it was me that brought him up'. But David is a grown man now and he makes his own decisions, there's nothing I can do about the way he feels. The trouble with Mum is she talks before she thinks things through and she does say some very hurtful things.

I eventually found myself being attracted to other men and I kept thinking, 'This shouldn't be happening'. I thought I was in love again a couple of times but they were just diversions. I was getting so bored at home. Roy was working very hard, he didn't seem to realise anything was wrong between us. I was playing table tennis for the BBC and I thought, 'I'll just have a few wild flirtations'. By this time I was in the teleprinting department which had close links with the news room. David Coleman was a reporter there in those days and he was very dishy. He was a great runner and he used to run to work but I only ever admired him from a distance.

I often used to see audition tapes and I remember the presentation organiser David Wilmot was watching one that Ray had done. I was in the studio when David was playing back Ray's tape and when I watched a bit of it I said, 'He's fantastic'.

The next thing that happened was that I popped my head round the door of the presentation office one day, and Ray was sitting there. BBC 2 was due to start in the north. Ray was coming in as an announcer and he was also going to do some trails promoting BBC 2. Margaret Davies, who was the senior secretary in the announcer's office said, 'Alma this is our new announcer Ray Moore'. I looked at him, he looked at me and I just remember my insides literally turning over, it was as instant as that. We both knew that something remarkable had happened.

Over the next few months Ray was doing record programmes, and I was Recorded Programmes Librarian which was a lovely job. Until then there had only been a very small library which wasn't very well organised and I was building it up. He'd come in for records and I was just aware of him all the time. I've always been a flirt but I didn't really know it was flirting. I just thought of it as being friendly. Then I moved jobs to work as the clerk in the television studio which was attached to the announcer's office. Quite often Ray and I were working on our own. The clerk had to prepare a skeleton script and then the announcer would sit by the desk and dictate the final version.

It was shift work and we were often together, just on our own for quite long periods. It became a very precious time, it was wonderful but pretty fraught because we could see it was getting serious and we didn't know what to do about it. If anything.

[3]

Ray and I both knew, right from the beginning, that we'd fallen in love and that it was no casual affair. We felt incredibly happy though at the same time frightened at the enormity of our feelings. We could never see each other at all at weekends but we just used to snatch any moment we could to be together. We'd often go at lunchtime to the Chinese restaurant in Piccadilly which was near the BBC. We were always trying to be careful not to be seen too much together, because there were so many gossips at work. When Ray's programme was over, we'd sit and talk in the studio and then some nights he'd walk me down to the bus station. He was just in my mind all the time, whatever I was doing, day and night. After a few months we really realised we couldn't bear to be apart. I bought him a little St Christopher's charm and had the date June 1st 1966 engraved on it, because that was the day we admitted to each other that we'd fallen hopelessly in love.

He had a flat in Manchester and going back with him for the first time to his flat was very fraught. It was just something we had to do but once we'd made love there was no turning back. He used to get very upset because I was married and had a child. We were both worrying about what we were doing to David. When I think back to those early days, Ray must have had doubts about whether or not he was doing the right thing, getting so committed to a married woman who was nine years older than me. By this time I wasn't having any kind of marital relationship with Roy because I can only be committed to one person at a time. There was absolutely nothing I could do about it.

It was very difficult for Roy, very hurtful; what I was doing was awful of me but I don't think he suspected things were as bad as they really were. When I finally, actually said to him I was unhappy and I wanted to split he was devastated. The whole story just came tumbling out and he was extremely hurt, angry and upset. It was the end of his world and I'm sure he wanted to hit me. He wanted us to go to marriage guidance and I went first on my own but the woman was hopeless, she said all the wrong things. I just felt so angry when I came out.

It was such a huge decision to walk out of my marriage. Obviously, if I left my husband for Ray, then Ray couldn't carry on working in Manchester. It might be different today, but twenty-five years ago it would have been impossible. I was just crying all the time, feeling guilty and worrying about David. Ray said, 'It's too awful what we're doing, we can't go on'. We decided that we'd stop seeing each other outside work but I couldn't cope with that, it was making me ill. I said to Ray, 'I can't stand it, I want to be with you.' We couldn't bear to be apart. Ray went back to Liverpool for a weekend once and he wrote me a card saying, 'Darling Alma, I miss, miss, miss, miss you and yearn for Monday and you. I long to see your nose wrinkle when you laugh and feel the shiver go up my spine when you make love to me with your eyes. Yes I'm wild about my beautiful Alma'.

Once he got terribly annoyed with me. We were doing a recording with a group that used to sing 'Wide Eyed and Legless' and during rehearsals we all went to a little sandwich bar. I was chatting to the lead singer about music and how the group had started. It was just the two of us and afterwards Ray was actually very angry with me. I said, 'You're jealous'. I was quite flattered, I thought, 'He really does love me.' He was actually still feeling very insecure about everything. We used to get all the stars coming to the BBC in Manchester to do 'Pop North' with Ray. Englebert Humperdinck came when he was still Gerry Dorsey and sang with the Northern Dance Orchestra and so did Tom Jones. He was very sexy, very macho but he didn't take any notice of me. I was too old for him, he was only interested in the younger ones. Ray and I were both very star struck and I just thought it was a magical world.

At home, I was still cooking for Roy and trying to do the normal household tasks but there was a strained atmosphere all the time. We were still desperately trying to put on a show for David who was only eight at the time. We'd argue and David would get upset. But there is no doubt about it, that the thing between Ray and me was unstoppable. The whole affair wouldn't have happened if it had been any other way, because we weren't irresponsible people. He kept saying, 'We must stop,' but we couldn't. I kept thinking, 'I can't be doing such a horrible thing'. We certainly weren't doing anything lightly, it was a very serious commitment. I was very aware of what I was doing and so was Ray.

I heard an interview recently with Enoch Powell. He was being asked if he regretted making his famous speech about rivers of blood and he said, 'There are some decisions in life that are already made for you.' And when I look back to when I first met Ray, that's exactly how I feel but I know that till the day he died he felt a huge burden of guilt about taking me away from David.

The fact that we were both working at the BBC made everything even more difficult. We both knew that there was a lot of gossip about us. It was understandable but I absolutely hated it. In the end, everything got so much on top of me, I just disappeared one day. I felt I had to be away from everybody, without people looking at me or talking behind my back. I had this great feeling of eyes watching me, whispers going all round the offices and I couldn't cope with that. I also wanted to get away from home, because the atmosphere was so awful and I knew it was my fault. Roy had done nothing wrong, he was a lovely man, he still is. One day I just packed one little bag and I left and after work I went round to see my mother. I said, 'Mum, I've left Roy. Can I come and stay with you for a while?' and she said, 'No, you can't'. Roy had already been round to tell her that I'd left home so she knew what was happening but it had come as a terrible shock to her. Roy and I had been keeping up such a good pretence, that nobody suspected things were so bad between us. I can never forget that at a time when I desperately needed help, she turned me away. But I do forgive her. We all do what we think is right at the time. I hope she forgives me too.

Ever since that happened I've always said to David, 'If you're in trouble at any time, whatever you've done, right or wrong, always come and tell me. And we'll sort it out somehow'. After I'd left Mum I felt so upset, I just didn't know which way to turn. In the end, I went to stay with Ray for a couple of days and then I felt I had to get right away even from him. He said, 'Why don't you go to Southport for a while?' So that's what I did. Ray took me to the station and when I got there I found a little bed and breakfast place, just between Lord Street and the sea, and I stayed there for two days. I walked round and round the streets with my head in turmoil, wondering if things would ever get sorted out.

I went back to Manchester after a couple of days and found another bed and breakfast place. My mother was still helping to look after David. She'd pick him up from school and take him home but she was totally against me, very hostile. She was criticising me to both Roy and David. David would repeat comments that Granny had said but Roy, to his eternal credit, told my mother that he didn't want to hear anything bad against me. He said that she certainly mustn't say anything critical of me to David. She was so beside herself with anger that she barged into the studio at Broadcasting House one day and hit Ray over the head with her handbag. She felt I'd brought disgrace on the family. She found it all difficult to cope with and she minded terribly about the neighbours finding out. Ray and I shed many a tear during that period. His hair started to come out with all the worry, it was as traumatic as that.

We knew though, beyond any doubt, that we wanted to spend our lives with each other. Ray said to me, 'Now we've decided to be together, you must come and meet my mother and father'. He took me to his parents' home in Liverpool and understandably they weren't very pleased about what was happening. His family are very down-to-earth working-class people. His mother is a very intelligent lady. They never said anything against me to Ray but obviously they weren't happy about the situation. They'd have much preferred him to be bringing home some young lady who wasn't married. His mother said, 'I disagree totally with what you're doing. You shouldn't be leaving your husband and your son'. I kept crying and I can remember her saying, 'Oh, for goodness sake stop crying'. I've always been a crier. I used to cry a lot as a kid whenever I was told off. I seemed to be upset all the time but I just knew there was no way I could go against this feeling I had for Ray.

I tried to explain to David, as well as I could to a child of eight, that I was very unhappy. I said that if I stayed, I would only make him and his Daddy unhappy as well. Looking back it makes me feel awful. But if I'd stayed, our marriage would have just trundled on in a bleak kind of way. Eventually David would have left home and Roy and I would have been left on our own. We would have been tied together with nothing between us, just a shell of a marriage. It was Roy who first told

David that we were splitting up. He used to take him swimming every week to Irlam baths and that's where he plucked up courage to tell him. He said we weren't getting along any more and we'd decided to be apart. He also said I was seeing somebody else, and in his young mind David thought of Ray as this man who was stealing his mother away from him.

I honestly don't know how I managed to leave David, but the power of the love I felt for Ray just took me over. Everybody was warning me about him, saying, 'Don't forget Ray is an ambitious young man, you're nine years older which is an awful lot. You'll go to London together, but soon he'll get tired of you. He'll leave you for somebody younger.' I knew they could be right but it just didn't make any difference.

Doing what I did does make you understand people better. Before it happened to me, if any other mother had done the same thing I'd have said 'What a bitch' without thinking what that person had been through. I felt wicked. I was doing all the things I didn't like in other people. I'd told lies, been unfaithful, I was leaving my husband and child. I'm not a rotten person and neither was Ray but we did cause upset to a lot of dear people. I don't judge other people now. I don't take sides. Roy said, 'Have you thought what might happen? You're going to London, he may leave you. And you'll be lost'.

Roy was understandably very bitter, and in the end he said to me, 'Why don't you just go away, leave us alone, get out of our lives?' He thought that if I went away it would be too upsetting for David just to see me now and again. I said, 'No, I can't do that. I love my son'. Then I kept wondering if Roy was right, if I'd do less harm if I just totally disappeared. I wondered if it would be the least damaging thing for David to have a totally clean break. I talked about it to a friend of mine at work called Kathy Murray and the advice she gave me still rings in my head. I just thank God for it. She said, 'Alma, whatever you do, keep

Left: Alma and her sister Audrey King. Their mother made all their dresses

Below: Alma's parents

Above: Ray's family on the beach at Port St Mary, Isle of Man

Left: Alma aged 14, her mother and her two sisters, Aunt Nell and Aunt Kate, in Blackpool, 1947

Below: Ray and his father checking a few points, Liverpool, 1980

Left: Alma and Kathy Taylor (now Murray), 1963. She gave Alma the best advice when she left home and is still a dear friend

Below: Alma and her first husband, Roy Mather, 1965

Left: Alma and Charlie Dawson in Southern Ireland

The young Alma King with Roy's pride and joy

The BBC Manchester Annual Dance in the Grand Hotel, Manchester, 1950. *From left to right:* Joan Whelan, Charles Hickey, Alma King, Jack Robson, Kathy Evans and her boyfriend

Ray broadcasting

The honeymoon in Jersey, 1969

Above: The studio – Ray's second home

Left: Alma in her composing days

Above: Ray auditioning for newsreader at the BBC

Right: Ray at the start of his professional career

Below: ATV Birmingham

Right: The French singer Minouche and Ray in Monte Carlo, 1969

Below: Terry Wogan and Ray in Broadcasting House, London. They were happy in each other's company

in touch with David. It won't be easy at first but time will be a healer. You'll still have a relationship with him and God willing, a loving relationship. But if you just disappear out of his life, you'll find it very difficult to ever get back. He'll be so hurt, he'll probably never forgive you'. She also said, 'He may resent you for a while but in time it will get better'.

I just clung to Kathy's words. I believed that what she had said was true. I kept hanging on to the hope that one day, if I tried really hard and never gave up, it would be all right between David and me. I know there was a period when he was very unhappy, when he hated me and Ray. The headmaster at his junior school was a super guy and he knew what had happened. He used to take David one side and ask him how he was. David hated him doing it because he just couldn't help the tears welling up in his eyes.

Ray and I talked things over and he said, 'Look, the best thing I can do now is to hand in my resignation'. He managed to get a three-month contract in London so that we wouldn't be destitute when we got there. The number two at the BBC in Manchester in those days was a man called John Reid who was a lovely man. He was president of the BBC Club and I was Honorary Secretary so I knew him well. He was like a father figure to me.

When I left, he wrote such a sweet letter on September 11th 1967 and it meant so much to me. I felt everybody thought we were mad and his kindness helped me such a lot. In his letter he said, 'It is sad that you are leaving us and sadder that it has to be like this. But now that you have made up your mind, I would like to say that I sincerely hope it will prove to be for the best and that you will find stability and happiness. If ever you want, in more settled times, to work again for the BBC, I will give the idea my full support. We shall miss you.' He never *said* anything to either of us, but Ray always believed that later it was

John Reid who was responsible for getting Ray the job in London that he really wanted. It was the job of news reader and announcer with what used to be called the Home Service. In those days, every announcer worked on all networks, so Ray was also working for the old Light Programme and the Third.

When he finally started doing that he was absolutely thrilled. He used to say he felt he'd been born to read the news on the Home Service. In the weeks before we went to London, I was still living in digs in Manchester. The night before we were due to leave finally, Ray did his last programme of a series called 'Pop North' in Manchester and Alan Price was on the bill. He said he was travelling back to London on the overnight train. We told him we were going to London together the day afterwards and he said, 'Travel back with me tonight'. It sounded very exciting but in the end we didn't. We said we'd better wait till the following day because we hadn't got a proper suitcase. Ray had got one that was falling to bits and, I'd just got the overnight bag I'd left home with.

In the morning we went into Lewis's which was just opposite the BBC. Ray trundled his old battered suitcase into the shop and we bought a big new one for £10. We transferred all our things from the old case into the new one and walked out of the store. Ray was carrying this huge, overloaded case filled with everything we had in the world. Just as we got through the main doors on to the pavement, the handle broke. There were clothes and books scattered everywhere. It seemed like a terrible omen. Ray went straight back to change it for another suitcase and we went off to get the train to London. I felt I wanted to get away, I couldn't bear being in Manchester at that time, feeling guilty and thinking every finger was pointing at us. The things in the suitcase mostly belonged to Ray because I had very little. I came away from home with nothing. I left my wedding and engagement ring behind because I didn't feel I had any right to have them.

Ray and I got on the train and part of me felt a sense of relief at having finally got away, but the rest of me was feeling absolutely wretched. People had always thought I was very together. I had a nice job, a little car, a lovely son, I was married to a good man and I was turning my back on it all.

Ray and I were both nervous, but we also had a great sense of stepping out, into something new. The future seemed exciting and I was with Ray, which I wanted more than anything else in the world. We didn't talk much on the train, but he sat with his arm round me for the whole journey. We just kept thinking, 'We're together and on our way to London,' and it didn't seem to matter that we'd nowhere to live, hardly any money.

From the moment I first met Ray, we always had great fun and that's really what I needed. Life's got to be fun. We got off at Euston, got a taxi to Paddington and we just walked the streets, looking for somewhere to stay the night. The money that landlords wanted for the most appalling places seemed terrible to us, we just couldn't believe it. But eventually we found one room we could just about afford in Sussex Gardens, near Paddington station. We desperately needed to get in somewhere and have a rest, rather than carting this suitcase round London. Ray was working the next day so he had to get some sleep. He often used to say, 'Alma, do you remember that awful first room we had, and how there was always that stale smell of somebody else's cooking?'

Ray owed a lot of money to the tax man because he wasn't organised about money in those days. I had a bit of money since Roy had been very fair. He'd divided our account at the bank and given me half which came to £216 19s 3d in old money. He was so exact about everything. In the letter he wrote to me he said, 'This of course will be less five shillings for the cheque book'.

Ray didn't want me to touch that money and we spent about

a month just going round from one horrible place to another to find different cheaper rooms. I didn't know London at all and when I was on my own and Ray was working, I felt like a lost soul.

One really depressing Friday night, Ray said, 'I'm going to give Joe Fessey a ring'. Joe was a lovely Cockney who used to work at the BBC in Manchester as a wire man. He'd always told us if ever we were in London, he'd put us up for a few days. We rang him up and he said if we went to the BBC Club he'd meet us there, which he did. He took us back to his little flat in Pimlico, let us have his single bed and he slept on a camp bed in the kitchen.

Ray and I slept in Joe's single bed for about two months and that whole period was very strange. I just felt very odd. Nothing was permanent, it was like living in transit. The only nice thing was that Ray and I were together, and in the end we managed to rent a studio flat in Blackheath. When he first suggested looking there, I said, 'Why on earth have we got to live in Blackheath?' But he'd set his heart on it. It just seemed a magical place to him. We took a little single-decker bus and went out to Blackheath together where we found this lovely big airy studio room.

After we'd been there for a few weeks we heard that Roy was going to come down to London to talk to us, perhaps to try and persuade me to go back. It sounds dreadful now, but we just didn't want to go over and over the old ground. We called to see Joe one day and he told us that we'd just missed Roy. He'd got our new address from Joe and I was terrified to death. Ray felt there might be a fight if he and Roy met. We couldn't face it and we moved into a bed and breakfast for the night so we wouldn't see him. I think Roy had a kind of love-hate feeling for me by this time. He did go to Blackheath but we weren't there of course, and when we got back all my clothes were in our flat. Roy had brought them over in the car from Salford, persuaded the caretaker to let him in and left them.

Before I'd walked out of my marriage Roy and I had terrible rows. He kept saying, 'How can you be so cruel, don't the last eight years count for anything?' He always said he still loved me and then he'd say, 'Think what you're doing to David'. The guilt is still with me, it will stay with both Ray and me forever. We were always conscious of what we'd done, how much hurt we caused. After he was grown up David and Julie had a couple of sessions with Ray and me talking things over. It was good for David and the four of us just cried and cried. He wanted to know what had really happened, why I'd wanted to leave his father. I told him that even before I met Ray, Roy and I had grown apart and that when Ray came along I just fell madly in love. David's never ever said, 'How could you have left me, Mum?' but he would have been quite justified if he had. I think he feels now that I was right to leave, that in the end, though he was unhappy for a long time, he gained from knowing Ray. The four of us always went on holiday together and we had some wonderful times together. Somebody said to David, 'Isn't it boring going on holiday with your Mum?'. David said, 'No it's great. Mum and Ray are as daft, if not dafter than we are'.

In London I felt very vulnerable, I felt all the time that I was leaning on Ray. I just loved him so much. I only felt safe when he was there and I could touch him and he'd hold me tight. London seemed so huge, a bit frightening. I'd only been there twice before and only for the day. I went once when I was applying to go on a make-up course at Television Centre in Shepherd's Bush, though in the end I didn't get accepted.

In those early weeks I just wanted to be with Ray. When he was there, I felt everything was all right. In the evenings though, sometimes we'd have quiet periods when we'd both be thinking hard. After all, Ray was a young man with all his career ahead of him. He must have felt concerned at times knowing that he wasn't free any more. I'd sit and think about what I'd done to David and how much I'd hurt Roy. There were a lot of tears from both of us. Then in December, just after I'd sent all his Christmas presents, David wrote to me. I read this little letter which ended, 'Mummy, I wish you would come home. Daddy has been very upset and so have I. We both still love you very much.' I said to Ray, 'I can't cope with this, I'll have to go back'.

Ray took me to Euston station and we were just desolate. We both thought that this was the end for us; but as soon as I got back to Salford I knew it was the wrong thing to have done. It put Roy in a terrible position. I felt I couldn't sleep in our bedroom with him, but David had a room with twin beds in it and I slept there. But it was just a mistake to have gone back, the whole thing felt wrong. I felt trapped, I couldn't wait to escape.

David was always a confident little boy, a leader. A small gang of children used to play in the street and he was always the one who used to tell the others what to do. But all children have a vulnerable spot deep within them. Roy was very worried that the whole thing might affect David's schooling, that he'd fail his exams, but thank goodness in the end he did pass to go to the grammar school. I still feel dreadful at returning and then leaving him a second time but I knew beyond any doubt that going home to Salford wasn't the right answer for any of us.

The first day that Roy went to work after I'd got back I left him a goodbye note. I took my things and I tried to explain to David in a simple way that I'd always keep coming to see him. I was crying and he was crying. I took him to Roy's mother's house and I left him there. I tried to explain to her how I felt but I don't think she understood. Then I just got the bus into

Manchester and caught the train back to London. I knew then that it was final, that I would never return.

Ray had absolutely no idea that I was travelling back to him. I got to our rented flat in Blackheath, he came home to find me there and we had a passionate reunion. I started going back to Manchester every month to be with David though he said he didn't want to see me. But I persevered. I'd usually travel back on Friday nights. I'd take David into Manchester on the Saturday and we'd have a meal and go to the cinema. Sometimes we'd get a train to Cheshire, take a packed lunch and just walk. Other times we'd go fishing even in the pouring rain because David loved fishing, and he taught me how to take the hook out of the fish's mouth.

It was often difficult in the early days because he was still upset. When I saw him I'd give him a hug and he'd stand quite stiff and stand-offish. It always worried me going back to Salford because, though I desperately wanted to see David, I didn't want to see any neighbours. I used to walk down my mother's street as everybody peered through their curtains at me. I'd hold my head up high and pretend I didn't care and think, 'Oh to hell with them'. Gradually the visits got easier. But then, when I was back in London I'd suddenly see a nine year old with fair hair and every child was David.

It was soon after I'd come back to London that we decided that we must save up enough for a deposit and buy a place of our own. I started doing holiday relief in the gramophone library at the BBC. I knew everybody there because I'd often talked to them on the telephone from Manchester. We used to live on my wages and we saved Ray's money. We found a lovely little garden flat in a new purpose-built block. It was called The Priory because it was built on the site of an old priory. The day we moved in we were so happy though we'd hardly any furniture. We rented a dormobile. I was driving, with Ray sitting on the front seat, clutching all my plants. If any of the neighbours saw us moving in they must have thought we were very odd, because the only furniture we had was a bed and a rocking chair. Ray always used to sit on the rocking chair to watch the news on television. Then, when the news was over, Ray insisted I sat in the chair whilst he sat on the floor.

The flat had beautiful French windows, opening on to the garden and we just couldn't believe we were there. We didn't have any garden chairs so we just used to sit on the step.

Behind The Priory was a tennis club with lots of courts. In the evenings when the summer came we used to walk round saying, 'Isn't it posh?' But eventually the day came when we joined the club and we played tennis on those courts.

By this time Roy was suing me for divorce. In those days, before the case could go through, a private investigator had to come round to our flat and see we were sharing a bed. When he came over, I thought, 'This is so sordid, it can't be happening to me'.

There was nothing in the world Ray and I would have liked more than to bring up David, but there was no way I could take David away from his father. Roy loved him so much and I'd caused him such a lot of hurt. I just knew I couldn't apply for custody. So when the case came to court I didn't attend. I know everybody thought it was awful but I just couldn't bear to go and to say, 'No I'm not applying for custody of my son'. I didn't go to court for the wrong reasons. I didn't go because I was worried about what people would think about this woman who wasn't fighting to keep her own child.

Roy had now met his young lady, who was a lot younger than him. She was only nineteen and she worked in the bank. I felt relieved but upset because she was looking after my son and, though I had absolutely no right to, I felt quite jealous when he told me he was getting married again.

I still feel love for Roy. We had some good years together, part of me will always belong to him. Ray used to say, 'That first marriage, that commitment will always be with you.' When there's a child there is a permanent bond and Roy and I produced this wonderful son. When we meet today he still always kisses me on the lips.

David must have had very confused feelings at this time. His stepmother was quite hard on him at times, very very strict. I know that later, when David was courting Julie, there were some very upsetting times. But to be fair, I have to give great credit to her for the input that came from her and Roy in helping make David as he is today. He's just a smashing bloke. When he was a little boy he called her Mam and then he changed to Anne but he's always called me Mum.

David's got an awful lot of his father in him, so many of his mannerisms and he's got my enthusiasms. I'm a jack of all trades and master of none. If David wants to do something, he wants to do it right away. If I buy anything, I wear it there and then and David's like that. Ray would buy something and then hang it up in the wardrobe. I'd say, 'Why don't you wear it?' and he'd say, 'I have to get used to it first.'

After Ray and I had been living together for a few months, my father became very ill. The doctors thought he was going to die. Roy got in touch with the police, and they came round to the flat in the middle of the night and knocked us up. They said I should travel north as quickly as I could. Ray ordered a cab to take me to Heathrow and I got a plane to Manchester. I went straight to Ladywell Hospital and I was there before my mother arrived. She walked in a bit later and the first thing she said to me was, 'Look what you've done to your father.' She blamed me totally for his illness because she said I'd upset him so much.

He was very, very sick. He'd been a heavy smoker all his life and he had chronic bronchitis. He was the sort of man who never said much. Like the fathers in lots of northern families, he left everything to my mother. He handed over the money and she paid all the bills. In the end, he recovered which was a miracle and he lived for quite a few more years. I stayed in Manchester for a while and I suppose my father's illness in a way brought about rapprochement with the family. Till then my mother made Ray out to be an ogre. She painted a terrible picture of both of us to David.

Whenever Roy heard what she was doing he went round to her house and tried to stop her saying these awful things. He said he wanted David to grow up without bitterness and then to make his own decisions. Roy couldn't have done more and I still feel guilty about him. If he'd been a rotter it would have been easier. He didn't deserve to be made so unhappy. He was very angry with David once because David had heard from my mother that Ray was working for the World Service and that we were going abroad for a while. David said, 'Good riddance to them both'. It would have been so easy for David to become bitter and twisted and the fact that he didn't is entirely due to Roy.

After the divorce, Ray kept saying, 'Will you marry me?' I said 'no' for a long time because I was afraid that the magic would go away if we got married. He was such a caring, passionate lover, very exciting. He just always thought of the other person first. He was desperate to care for me. He took the responsibility very seriously. He actually used to have nightmares that he wasn't looking after me properly. Apart from his family, he'd never been responsible for another adult in his life. I think he felt a bit like a young mother, taking her baby home for the first time.

One day I suddenly felt that it would be good to get married, and we decided to fix the date for May 9th 1969. We'd upset the family so much that we couldn't see it being a happy day if they all came, so we didn't ask them. We decided that the wedding would be just for us, it was going to be our day. In the end my mother came to adore Ray. If she met anybody new the first thing she would ever say would be, 'Ray Moore is my son-in-law and he's a lovely man'. I'd say to her sometimes, 'You didn't use to feel like that'. But she'd just say, 'Oh, that was a long time ago'.

Joe Fessey and his lady friend were our two witnesses and the only guests. I wore a close-fitting black and white dress, with a high neck and a white sleeveless overcoat. We got married in Greenwich Register Office and Ray hired a mini cab to pick us up. When it arrived it was filthy and the spare wheel was on the back seat. I thought I'd probably arrive covered in oil and grease. Afterwards, we'd booked a table for four at the Marquis in Mount Street. The song writer Jimmy Kennedy had taken Ray there once and he was knocked out by it. We all had a super lunch and when we came out of there we went to Trader Vic, the bar at the Hilton. We spent our first married night together at Berners Hotel and then we flew off to Jersey. When we woke up in London that first morning we were listening to Bruce Wyndham's programme on the radio. He said that two friends of his were on their honeymoon in Jersey and he'd arranged for the hotel to give them an early morning call. He thought we'd flown off the night before but there we were lying in bed together listening to every word he was saying about the trick he thought he was playing on us.

Ray was still part of a team of announcers at the BBC and he was loving it. It seemed the gods were smiling on us. I was still going back to Manchester once a month to see David. I'd stay with my mother because after my father was so ill things gradually got a bit better between us. Roy would bring David round in the car to Grandma's. He'd always say, 'Are you all right?' He was still concerned for me.

When I got back to Blackheath and the flat after a weekend in Salford, Ray would very casually say, 'Did you see Roy when you were there?' I know he always felt a bit jealous and worried whilst I was away.

[4]

In the beginning Ray and I were very poor, we worked our way up and then we appreciated everything we got. We always knew that the BBC might not renew his contract so we never lived up to our income. Ray just stashed everything away in the building society but we still lived well and did lovely things. Ray would suddenly say, 'Come on let's go to the Connaught, let's have a wonderful meal'.

We always left notes for each other. When Ray went freelance, we had to keep a diary with all his bookings. He called it our bible and we'd write little messages to each other on it. If we'd invited a few friends round for drinks Ray would write 'Party' in the diary. When I saw that I'd write, 'It's not a party Ray, just friends coming for drinks'. I was always the practical realist while he loved everything to sound glamorous. There was lots of communication between us which is the making of a good relationship.

After Ray and I had been in London for about a year, David and I started going off on holidays together. The first year I took him to a hotel in Southport and we went fishing together, swimming, I taught him how to play tennis. Later we went to Anglesey and one year I took him to a little sailing school on the Isle of Wight. We had to learn to rig a boat, go out and sail it and then come back and derig it. We had a marvellous time together. It was a lovely place, right on the creek. Everybody used to eat together and there was a mess room with a little bar. David thought this was absolute magic because you could go and help yourself to a drink whenever you wanted and just enter it in the book. It went on your bill at the end of the week, of course. But I always remember how David loved going to get himself a Coke and saying, 'This is great, Mum'.

I concentrated one hundred per cent on David whilst we were together but I used to ring Ray nearly every night. I always talked to David a lot about his father, and in a nice way, because I didn't want him to think I was trying to alienate him. I also felt very grateful to Roy because he never did anything wrong and he behaved with the utmost fairness to me. At the end of the holiday, it was hard saying goodbye to David, particularly when we'd been so close, but I never cried and neither did he. He wasn't a little boy who showed his emotions much, he was very self-contained on the outside. I was always upset but I was very lucky because I was going back to Ray. Some women in similar circumstances after a family break-up have to go back to a lonely, empty flat.

In the early years, Ray and I talked about having children but I said to Ray, 'I've left David; we still don't know whether we've totally messed up his life or not. So how dare we think of having another child?' I also felt that when David came to see us, I wanted him to be the only one. I didn't want him to feel he was having to compete for attention with somebody else or have to share us. It meant we could devote all our interest and care to him and I believe we made the right decision. In our dotage, Ray and I sometimes said, 'Wouldn't it have been interesting to see what a child of ours would have looked like?' but we didn't have regrets. If you decide to do something, you've got to believe in it and not forever be looking back. I think it made our relationship even stronger because we cared for each other in a child-like way. In a lot of ways, neither of us ever grew up. In my heart, I've always stayed the girl from a two-up two-down in a street in Salford and Ray was still the little lad from

Liverpool. And also on the selfish side, Ray and I wouldn't have had the life we had if we'd had the ties of children. He'd ring up at a moment's notice to say, 'Come for a drink, come for dinner,' and I'd drop everything and go. At first people thought it strange that Ray always brought his wife along, but that's how we started off in the early days and how we carried on.

I think initially it was partly because I felt very lost when Ray wasn't there. I wanted to be with him as much as I could, and when he was around I always felt confident. Having been brought up all my life in one small community, where I couldn't walk down the street, without seeing someone to speak to, I suddenly found myself in a place where I didn't know anybody. We also both felt that having been through so much to be together, we didn't want to waste a minute. I'm sure people rather laughed at us behind our backs. In London men don't bring their wives along, they'd much rather stand at the bar and complain that their wives don't understand them. I think a lot of people thought I came along because I was keeping an eye on Ray. I was quite shy and if there were any strangers there I used to say, 'Ray, don't leave me standing on my own'. He'd say to me, 'Treat it like work, treat it like an interview, just ask them questions about themselves and you'll end up getting their life story'. He was quite right and that's what I did.

In the beginning Roy didn't want David to come and stay with Ray and me. He said that when David was old enough to decide for himself he could make his own decisions. The first time he met Ray was just before we went to the Isle of Wight. David came to London on the train and he stayed with us in Blackheath before we went off on holiday. Ray said to him, 'David, I'm not your stepfather. I'm Ray'. Roy had never criticised Ray to David which left him free to make up his own mind. It would have been terrible if his young mind had been poisoned but thankfully it wasn't, though my mother did her best.

When David came to stay with us, we allowed him to accept us or not. He was never a particularly tactile person, but we would always give him a big hug.

Ray of course went overboard trying to make him feel welcome. We just wanted him to become part of our life, and gradually he and Ray grew to love each other. When he was about seventeen, he came down on his motorbike. Ray used to sit on the pillion and David would take him to Broadcasting House. If it was a hot evening and Ray was home, the two of them would sit outside with a beer and that's when they began to get close. They could really talk to each other and if ever David wanted to do anything Ray would say 'Have a go'. Recently I found a little note that Ray once left for us when David had taken me to a concert after he'd become ill. Ray had written, 'So we remembered where we lived then? Most wives seem to get home before dark. I suppose you'll say you ran into old friends? And who is that young man who brought you home and would he like a port? And another? Hope you had a lovely evening. Love you both to bits, Ray'.

When David started going out with Julie, they both came to spend a holiday with us in a village called Molland in Devon. We'd rented three little cottages with some friends and Ray said, 'David, I know you are going out with Julie but I don't want your father thinking we're encouraging anything he wouldn't approve of. I don't want you sleeping with Julie while you're here.' I laughed and I said, 'Ray this is silly,' but he was very serious. He said, 'I don't want anybody thinking old Ray's an easy touch. They're not sleeping together under my roof, I'm not having any place of ours getting the image of being a free house.' He really was very worried and we spent hours moving beds. I should think David and Julie laughed like drains behind our backs. Ray had a great puritanical streak and he was very concerned about what Roy might think. I was so pleased that David had a girl friend. They met at Buile Hill sixth form college and Julie's lovely. She used to be a senior clerk at the DHSS and she's got an awful lot of common sense. She comes out with some very profound thoughts.

After a while Ray said, 'We're doing all right, there's no need for you to work in the gramophone library any more,' so that was when I stopped. It left me freer to be with him. On his days off we'd get on a bus, go into the country and have a pub lunch. When he went freelance in 1973 he had to have someone to do the books, answer the phone and make appointments, so I took that over. He used to say, 'My freelance career wouldn't have taken off if it hadn't been for you'. I loved doing it and because I'd always worked at the BBC I understood how things were organised. Whenever people approached Ray about bookings he'd say 'Ring Alma,' and I bet sometimes before they'd spoken to me, they'd think, 'Oh God, that will be a nightmare'.

When we first came to London, Ray didn't like holidays. He was still unsure of himself. He'd got to London, he was broadcasting for the BBC and he didn't want to take time off. I kept saying, 'You need a break or you won't be able to carry on'. He said, 'I'm always afraid that if I go away I might not be able to do it when I get back.' He was always scared of his talent disappearing. Whenever people said to him, 'How do you do it?' he'd say, 'I don't know.' He was terrified it would be taken away from him and of course it was.

I thought I knew everything there was to know about Ray but in a way I'm still learning. In the end he agreed to have a break and our first holiday together was on the Isle of Wight. We stayed in a little guest house which was all we could afford. We booked full board and Ray used to say, 'Isn't it wonderful? Three cooked meals a day'.

We walked and walked in the morning and afternoon, and we liked to get really spruced up in the evening for dinner. We'd talk a lot and basically we were just happy with our own company. Over the years Ray came to love his holidays, but he loved getting home and he was always nervous on the first day back at work. He used to talk to the studio and even when he hadn't been away he'd greet it every morning. When he left, he'd say goodbye.

In the early days I listened to every broadcast that Ray ever did and he always used to ask me what I thought. Later we went on some marvellous working trips together, though Ray was always meticulous about paying for me. He did a series of hour-long star interviews which went out as specials on Radio 2 and which took us all over the world.

We were talking to a famous television personality one night in the BBC bar and I said, 'Ray's interviewing Julio Iglesias soon and I'm going with him'. The other chap who'd just interviewed him said, 'You won't get much out of him, he's a wooden top'. I said, 'Oh, crumbs and we're going all the way to Antwerp.' When I got Ray on his own I said, 'The interview is going to be hard work,' and I told him what I'd just heard. He said, 'I'll really make sure I do my homework then.' Julio was on tour and when we got to Antwerp with Ray's producer Denis O'Keeffe we had to get through all these flipping guards. One of his aides showed us into an area where the dressing rooms were and told us to wait.

We waited for absolute ages, getting more and more anxious. We could see it was getting nearer and nearer to the time Julio would have to go on stage and the interview had to be done before the performance. Denis O'Keeffe said, 'We're not going to get it'. Suddenly Julio walked in and he said, 'Hi. You're the guys from the BBC aren't you?' He was very tall, very brown and incredibly handsome. He tends to wear a lot of blue and he had a navy blue overcoat slung over his shoulders. Denis said, 'I realise you're due on stage at any moment,' and Julio said, 'You guys have come all the way from England to see me. You need plenty of time. We'll do the interview now.' Ray said, 'Isn't it nearly time for your performance?' and Julio said, 'The performance can wait.' He actually held up the show so he could do the interview.

Denis said, 'I'd like you to sit over here.' Julio said, 'I'll tell you where I'm going to sit,' and he sat me down on the sofa next to him. He said, 'We must see that Alma is comfortable.' He then did the whole interview holding my hand. I felt quite weak at the knees. He speaks very quietly and he has this wonderful accent. Television doesn't flatter him because he's far more charming and handsome to look at in real life. He gave a superb interview and afterwards Ray said, 'That has taught me never to listen to anybody else ever again.' We'd been so convinced that Julio really was going to be difficult. He kissed me goodbye and I nearly melted. We just floated away into the night and went off to have dinner.

The one interview that Ray realy wanted to do was with Frank Sinatra. He always felt that if he could just get to him and they could have a pie and a pint together then it would be okay. Ray adored Sinatra and so did Derek Mills who was Assistant Head of Radio 2. Derek and his wife Doreen used to give wonderful dinner parties at their house in Bromley. We'd have this marvellous food and chat and then the evening always ended upstairs in Derek's study when he'd put on all his videos of Sinatra. We often used to come back from their place as the milkman was putting the milk on the step and the birds were singing.

Denis O'Keeffe always does his homework thoroughly and he really thought Ray could get to Frank Sinatra if we all went out to Los Angeles. He also set up some other interviews as well just in case the big one didn't come off. When we got to Los Angeles we stayed at the Sportsman's Lodge just near Coldwater Canyon. Ray wasn't interested in gossip about who slept with whom. In his interviews he just wanted to talk about their music and why they'd written or sung a certain song. I spent most of my time lying on a sun lounger by the pool, because somebody had to be around just in case there was a phone call. The waiter would bring the telephone out into the garden and I just felt I was in one of those Hollywood movies that I used to see in Salford. We had to go to Lionel Ritchie's recording office in downtown LA to interview him, and then Ray did a programme with Albert Hammond who wrote 'It Never Rains In Sunny California' and 'Ninety Nine Miles to LA'. Ray was a great fan of song writers and Hammond was a lovely man.

Denis was burrowing away all the time trying to get to Sinatra. We knew that he was in his house in the hills above LA, that he actually was in residence. We just kept thinking all the time that it was going to come off because Denis was talking to the man closest to Sinatra. His minders had said they wanted a list of all the questions that Ray would ask him and this was telexed to the States before we left London. They were all about music and nothing to do with his private life.

In the end we didn't get the interview and Ray used to talk on his show in the mornings about his trek to LA and failure to meet Sinatra. He'd say, 'I know it would be fine if I could just get him in the Railway Tavern over a pint.' Listeners used to write in and say, 'I've written to Frank Sinatra, Ray, and told him what a lovely guy you are,' and it became an ongoing thing. I'm sure that when Sinatra arrives at the Golden Gates, Ray will be there waiting for him.

Frank Sinatra, Sammy Davis Jnr and Liza Minnelli gave a

concert at the Albert Hall after Ray had died and I went to see it. Ray had worked there so many times and when I first arrived and sat in my seat I could still hear his voice booming around the auditorium, 'Ladies and gentlemen, Miss World 19 . . .' There was a song called 'Sailor Boy' which had been written specially for Liza Minnelli and she did it so well, I shed a few tears. I thought, 'Ray would have adored this'. Sammy Davis told us how much he'd wanted to play *Phantom of the Opera* but they wouldn't let him. He said, 'I even said to the guys in charge, "Look fellas think of the money you'd save, you won't have to put a mask on me".'

Liza Minnelli and Sammy Davis were both introduced before they came on but nobody introduced Sinatra. He just sauntered on and the place was in an uproar. His wind has gone, he can't belt the songs out as he once did. He can't hold the long notes either, but he's still devilish, still got that special charm and you can forgive him anything. I'd asked Graham Lambourne who works for Radio 2 promotions to escort me and afterwards he drove me home. He opened the car door and kissed me on the cheek. I'd said, 'I don't want any money for the ticket, you're my guest,' but he said, 'No, Alma it's a lot of money.' He insisted on paying and as I got out of the car he gave me £50. I thought, 'If this had been in my mother's street and a young man was kissing me and giving me fifty quid, the tongues wouldn't half wag. There would be a face pressed at every window.'

I also went to see a Tom Jones concert and the only thing that upset me was some of the audience. Women of my age were going up to him giving him their knickers and he was mopping his brow with them. One woman gave him a very skimpy pair and he kissed them. He did the usual thing of throwing off his tie, undoing his shirt and he was sweating like a pig. He's quite chunky now and the trousers were pleated

[85]

round the waist but he still did the thrusting of the hips. It would be interesting to talk to those women – I should think a psychiatrist would have a field day. I just felt terribly embarrassed for them all.

Ray was associated with the early show on Radio 2 from 1980 but it didn't become the Ray Moore show until January 1984. At the beginning of 1982, he was doing three months on and one month off when somebody else would do it.

One night, we were at a party where there was a great mix of folk, a lot of BBC people. It was the farewell party for Peter Chiswell, the legendary producer. I was chatting to Charles McLelland who was Controller of Radio 2 at the time and another girl, Helen, a secretary who worked on the early show. Ray was at the other side of the room. Charles was talking about how it was unsatisfactory having the system of three months on, one month off. I thought, 'Hang on, he must be looking for somebody permanent.' I said, 'What about Ray?' Charles said, 'I thought he didn't want to do it permanently?' So I said, 'Have you asked him?' Going home that night I told Ray what had happened. A week later he was called into Charles's office. It was all sorted out, Ray got a contract and he was chuffed to bits.

From then on his alarm went off at 3.15 every weekday morning. Sometimes if he hadn't got any work till later in the day he'd come straight home and be back just after 8.00. He'd put the kettle on and bring me up a cup of tea. He'd sit on the edge of the bed and I'd say, 'How did the show go?' and he'd tell me all about it. He loved that programme and he had listeners right across the board. He worked on the BAFTA Awards programme and afterwards he came home all beaming and said, 'You won't believe this but Anthony Hopkins says he's a fan'. We also met Cilla Black once at a Variety Club lunch and she said that she'd started listening to Ray when she had her last baby and was feeding the baby in the early mornings.

I always went to the Miss World contest; it was so funny to see how our status changed over the years. In the early days Ray only used to do the opening announcement. The first time he did it we got to the Albert Hall, we'd never been before and we were a bit shy. Pete Murray and Michael Aspel used to do the commentary then and we were just two little hicks from the north. I was so interested seeing all the girls in their curlers – really you could do a whole programme on that backstage bit. Ray did the opening and then we left. We said, 'Oh mustn't it be marvellous to stay for the whole thing?'

Later Ray started to do the commentary in between, and it used to give him a terrific thrill to hear his voice booming round the Albert Hall. We then progressed to the stage where we'd have tickets to one of the boxes and there would be a buffet and champagne. And then finally we progressed to actually being invited to the Miss World Ball afterwards at the Grosvenor House Hotel. Mike Begg was the producer one year and Ray and I were very fond of him. He's extremely handsome and he turned up looking terrific. I looked down at his feet and he'd still got his gym shoes on. I said, 'Mike, why are you wearing those with a dinner suit?' He said, 'I forgot to pack my shoes. Anyway what the hell, these are comfortable.'

It was marvellous to be so much part of Ray's career, but it didn't keep me occupied all the time. Our local church has a little magazine and I spotted an advertisement saying 'Volunteers needed. If you've got four hours to spare, ring this number'. I rang and found out they were looking for volunteers at Greenwich Hospital. I went to the Voluntary Services Organiser for Greenwich Health Authority who is a witty lady called Kitty

Salmon. She asked me if there were any areas that I didn't want to work in. I said I didn't think I could work in the psychiatric unit.' She told me they needed people in speech therapy, so I had a trial period there and I absolutely adored it.

When I first went there I just trailed the chief speech therapist in everything she did. She could be assessing a very sick patient who'd just been brought in having had a stroke or be in out-patients, or on the wards. She gave me books to read and then I went to work on the wards on a one-to-one basis. I kept thinking, 'Here's me, not qualified or anything and they're allowing me to work with very sick people'.

Most of the patients I work with have had very bad strokes that have affected the speech areas of their brain. I spend time just trying to get them to recognise basic things like cup, spoon, comb. Sometimes I'll give patients a comb and they'll try to clean their teeth. Other times they know what an object is but they can't get the word out.

You get a lot of anger. Mostly I work with patients who can't speak. Now we're using American Indian hand talk which is very successful. Firstly the patients learn three gestures so they can communicate three basic needs, the lavatory, a drink, or food. It was formulated by an American Indian doctor Madge Skelly who'd been taught by her grandfather. When lots of different groups of Indians meet for pow-wows, they all have different languages so they use hand talk. I love the work and I get as much out of it as I'm giving. Later Ray paid for me to go on an Aids Counselling course and now I go and visit any Aids patient who wants a friendly understanding visitor.

When Ray became ill he was adamant I still went every Thursday. He said, 'Alma I insist you go and have a day away from me. We'll have the district nurse to come in and do my dressing'.

Throughout his illness he was still caring for me, I used to say, 'How will I ever manage without you?' and he'd say, 'You will and you mustn't sit and mope. You must not waste your life.' We talked about dying and I'd never thought I'd be able to talk about the one I loved dying but it got easier. You know it's going to happen and it's only another word.

[5]

Ray was better at expressing his thoughts than me. If we were talking about something and I wasn't really saying what I felt, he'd say, 'Come on, you must have an opinion'. He'd help me get my thoughts out and he used to say he'd learnt things from me. If I'd been ill and anybody said, 'How are you?', I'd always say 'Fine', because nobody wants to learn about your aches and pains.

When it came to the point where we found our lovely little house in Blackheath, Ray said, 'We can't afford it.' We talked to David about whether or not we could manage to buy it and he said, 'How much have you got in the building society?' When Ray told him, he said, 'Ray you can easily afford to buy this house and still live well.' Ray said, 'Oh, I hadn't thought of touching that money.' He looked on the money in the building society as a nest egg for a rainy day. David said that the money would be much better in bricks and mortar.

Ray always wanted to look after me, he got great pleasure from that. When he was on an early shift and I'd been at the hospital all day he'd prepare everything for supper. When I got home at 4.30, the table would be dressed, a glass of wine poured, he'd have roasted a chicken. He'd say, 'It's all ready' and we'd sit and have a drink before we ate. I'd say, 'You are good,' and he'd say, 'You've been working all day and look how often you have everything ready for me'. When he was ill and I was dressing the wound he was always saying, 'You shouldn't be doing this,' and I'd say, 'Remember how you looked after me after I had my hysterectomy?' He was like a mother hen, doing all the hoovering, the cooking – and broadcasting as well.

When I had my hysterectomy Ray was marvellous. He got all the books he could find and read up all about it. I was recuperating at home, I hadn't to do any lifting or anything strenuous and Ray did everything. I think I must have made his life hell at that period and when I look back I feel awful. I was very weepy, very moody. One minute I'd be all soppy and lovely and then five minutes later I'd be angry. He went out for a drink with David once and he said, 'Your mother's driving me bananas'. While I was recuperating at home, Ray's father died, so of course he had to go straight to Liverpool. He rang me every day and I was always in tears. He felt, quite understandably, that being the eldest, he must take charge and look after everybody but I behaved very badly. I said, 'Your father is dead. You can't do anything for him. Why won't you come home because I need you here'.

I put such pressure on him but of course he had to stay in Liverpool. It must have been awful for him, I was being totally selfish. And because his Dad came from the Isle of Man and he'd said he wanted to be buried there, they had all the problems about transporting the body. The whole thing was a nightmare.

He'd become so much closer to his Dad in the last few years of his life. We used to go up to Liverpool quite a lot to see the family and go out for a drink with him. I'd always go as well – I don't believe in this business of the men going to the pub and the women staying at home. Ray's Mum would never come because of the drink, she still had this fear of alcohol due to all those years when Ray's father was drinking too much. In the end, Ray managed to get her to have the occasional glass of champagne. He'd say, 'Come on Mum, it's good for your chest'. But she'd never go in the pub.

As a little boy Ray was always told what terrible places pubs were and he thought they must be dens of sin and iniquity. He finally screwed up enough courage to walk into one when he was about nineteen but he was terrified at the thought of what he might find. He saw men just standing around smoking and laughing and he couldn't believe what a bright friendly pleasant place it was. His Mum wanted to make sure her children didn't fall foul of alcohol, but both Ray and his brother Don got a taste for the drink. Ray's Dad was a very heavy drinker and for a few years things were bad. He left home, did casual work, slept in doss houses. He wasn't allowed to go home and he used to visit the children when they were playing in local parks. He couldn't get any lower and then he literally dragged himself up by his bootstraps. It must have been awful for Ray's Mum. She was left without much money, bringing up three children on her own. She had to pull them all through some very hard times, and just to keep body and soul together she had to go out to work for a time at Littlewoods Pools. It all affected Ray a great deal. He felt responsible for the others and then when his father returned after five years he resented this man coming back into the house. It's evidently very common in cancer cases, to find that something very traumatic happened in childhood.

Ray wanted everything to be lovely, everybody to be happy. He learnt as a child always to try and be nice. When parents are stressed, children realise from a very early age that if they get angry the parents will shout, 'I've not got time for you now'. They find that the best way to get love and praise is by being very good and helpful. Then in adult life, they grow up into terrific people who'll do anything for you. They never show any anger even when it's justified. In chronic cases they don't even feel anger any more, it's been completely suppressed and Ray was just like that. Also for a long time, he had this inner turmoil because of all the fears that had been instilled in him about the wrath of God. I can understand why Ray's Mum did it, she was just desperately trying to keep them all on the straight and narrow and her whole existence consisted of work. She said to me once, 'I've had a very hard life,' and she was just speaking the simple truth.

When Ray was ill, we were listening to a tape of a woman therapist talking about how parents under stress affect children. She said how important it was in later life to let that little child come out, to exorcise that child and the pain. She then talked about how parents can use religion to instil fear in a child and Ray said, 'God, she's hit the nail on the head'. Ray still had that little boy deep inside him and I don't think it ever totally escaped. Children like that suppress their own stress and it later can show up in ulcers, heart disease, cancer.

But a lot of Ray's drive and strength also came from his mother. She felt she had let God down, by not following her nursing career. When she was young she was a nursing sister at Walton hospital and she planned to go on and study tropical diseases. Then she met Ray's father Bill, fell in love and in those days if a girl got married, she had to leave nursing. During the bad times when Bill was drinking she felt that this was payment for her sin of abandoning nursing. Ray went against all his father's wishes, because his Dad desperately wanted him to have a good, respectable job. He himself had done all sorts of jobs to make money; at one time he was making coffins and he worked hours and hours of overtime so Ray could stay on at school to take his A levels. Ray tried to get a place at the London School of Economics which would have made his Dad so proud but he was turned down. He ended up working in the Dock Board Offices in Liverpool which he hated. One morning he was sitting there, thinking how ridiculous it was to be watching ships set sail around the world; he was stuck in a total rut.

He thought to himself, 'I'm free, I'm only nineteen years old, I ought to be going somewhere.' He started buying the *Stage* and saw that Oldham Rep wanted an assistant stage manager which is a good euphemism for dogsbody. He applied, he was a good-looking kid and the producer said, 'We need somebody straight away, can you start at the end of the week?' At first he didn't dare tell his father and when he finally did his Dad was appalled beyond belief. He felt Ray had reneged on an unwritten bargain. But his Mum stuck up for him, she recognised that the passion for work that had been in her was also in Ray and she encouraged him.

His father was a great reader, he loved words. When the kids had any discussions or disagreements he'd always say, 'Get the dictionary out, get the maps out.' He loved maps. So did Ray; he loved finding out about things and he had a great self-critical streak. When he was younger he felt that he was turning his back on God by getting drunk, going out with girls, being obsessed with sex. He started questioning everything, there was great turmoil in his mind about sex and religion. When he was a young actor he started keeping some journals. Before he died I said, 'Ray what shall I do with those journals?' and he said, 'Burn them' but I couldn't. I found them and read them recently and they upset me a great deal. Poor lamb, before I met him, he was a poor tormented soul. There was the lovely smashing Ray we all knew but there was also the other side which was full of doubt and guilt. In one of the journals he wrote: 'Sometimes I think I'm alive only to die. Some people are like that, whatever they do, their supreme achievement is death. Scott Fitzgerald was one, so were T. E. Lawrence and James Dean. Only in death was the magnitude of these men's humanity and genius for living revealed.' He always felt absolutely sure that he would die while he was still a young man and he did, but at least he died at the peak of what he was doing. Some of this feeling is reflected in the journal at the end of this book.

*   *   *

After he and I came to London he would get very anxious when we went back to visit the family in Liverpool. He loved them all so much, but he used to use the word claustrophobic. He felt trapped. He always had the terrible fear that he might never escape again. When we got there he'd wake up next morning and he'd say, 'I'm still here'. He'd have this strong feeling that he'd never got away. He was always quite excited about going back, but it was a strange mixture of apprehension and anticipation. When we got off the train at Lime Street, his Dad would be there waiting for us; you could see this face bobbing about in the crowds, with curly hair and a tear in his eye. He'd have a great beam on his face which would be shining. He always looked as though he had just been scrubbed. When he saw Ray they'd give each other a big hug.

Ray had had to put such effort in to getting rid of his Scouse accent. He had this irrational terror that when he got back to Liverpool the northern accent would come back and that the city would grab him and never let him go again. The fear gradually faded over the years and I hope that was because I helped make him feel more secure. When we arrived back in London, we'd get in a cab at Euston and Ray would have a big smile on his face. He'd lean back in the cab with his arm round me and he'd say, 'We're home now'.

He was very outgoing, he never felt alone anywhere. He'd just walk into the nearest pub and straight away be talking to people. He always knew his way around, even in places he hadn't been to before. I don't like being in strange places on my own, I haven't got that confidence. We used to talk and laugh such a lot and I'd tell him everything. I miss that terribly but I still tell him anyway. I just talk to him whenever I'm worried or unhappy and I do feel his presence around particularly in his study. He used to talk to the house.

Whenever we left to go out he'd say, 'Goodbye little house,

we won't be long, be safe.' When we got home he'd say, 'Hello, little house, we're back now, have you missed us?' Consequently I find that now I'm doing the same. I'm sure that a lot of people who've been bereaved find themselves doing and saying the same things that their partners did.

When Terry Wogan decided to leave radio and go to television a lot of Ray's friends assumed that he'd be offered the job and he was upset not even to be asked. He'd stood in for Terry so many times. Audiences loved Terry but Ray believed that the BBC shouldn't try and replace him. They were looking for another Terry Wogan but Ray thought they should reschedule the programmes, change the slots and have somebody who was quite different. He was very hurt but he always said, 'God closes one door and opens a row of cottages'. He also used to say, 'You can get much further forward by taking one step backward'. Ken Bruce of course got the job and he's a wonderful broadcaster but I know he got very depressed for a long time because he was expected to be another Terry Wogan.

Terry is delightful, very huggable. I could almost fall in love with him. Right from the beginning when Terry and Ray were working on Radio 2 there was always a good rapport between them; they've got the same sense of humour. Ray really loved Terry and I think Terry loved Ray. When they were on radio together they always had this funny chat between programmes.

They both used to talk about their wives but they'd never say our names. I could never get Ray to use the door handle, he'd just push the door open and leave a dirty mark so I was always wiping the paintwork. He'd say, 'The blackhand gang's been round again Terry!'

They both liked the same things, a nice meal with some nice friends and time to talk. Before Ray died we went over to Terry

Ray with Vic Damone and Charles McClelland

Pop Score – the 200th programme

The link with the Salvation Army became increasingly important

Radio 2 – bright and early

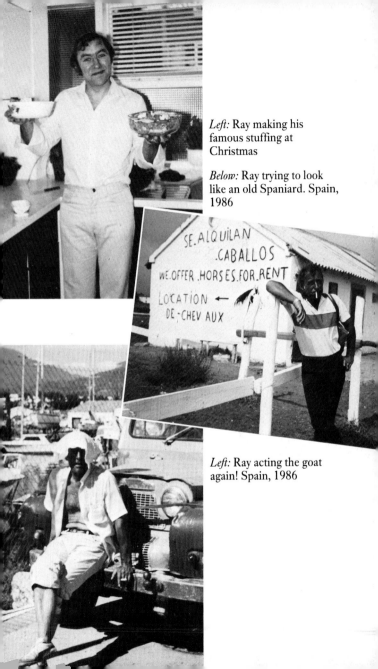

Left: Ray making his famous stuffing at Christmas

Below: Ray trying to look like an old Spaniard. Spain, 1986

Left: Ray acting the goat again! Spain, 1986

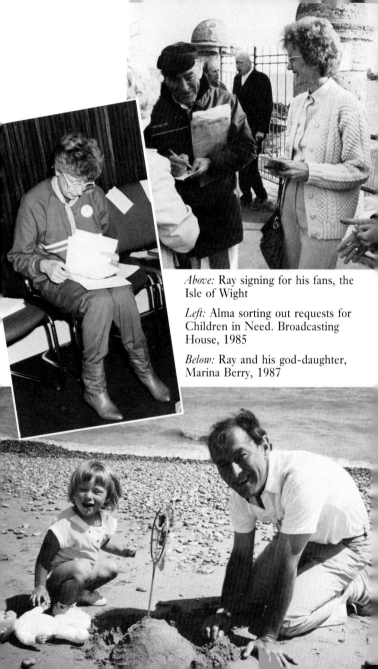

Above: Ray signing for his fans, the Isle of Wight

Left: Alma sorting out requests for Children in Need. Broadcasting House, 1985

Below: Ray and his god-daughter, Marina Berry, 1987

From left to right: Brenda Appleby, Alma, Kathy Murray, Kate Kenny in Strafford-upon-Avon, 1987

About to leave for the Charity in Concert version of *Mack and Mabel* at the Theatre Royal in Drury Lane, 1988. Ray was too ill to go, so he asked David to escort Alma

Joan Potter and Alma on board the France-England car ferry in May 1987. This was the last holiday in which Ray was really fit

Making a home movie

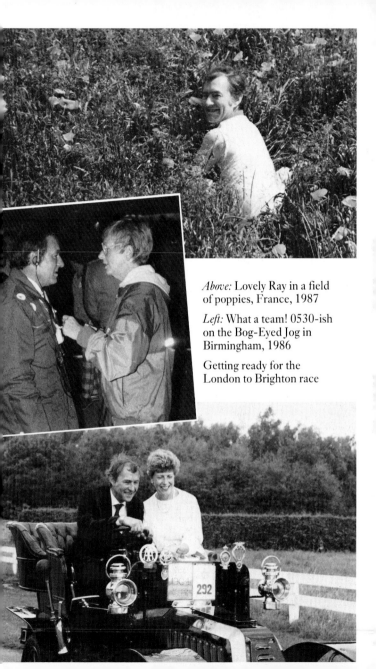

Above: Lovely Ray in a field of poppies, France, 1987

Left: What a team! 0530-ish on the Bog-Eyed Jog in Birmingham, 1986

Getting ready for the London to Brighton race

Left: At Cherry Cottage, 1985

Below: Ray enjoying a relaxing sail during Cowes Week, 1987

Left: Ray on a walking holiday in Devon

and Helen's house for lunch, it was a lovely summer's day. I was in and out of the pool and wonderful food kept appearing. Terry had put Ray next to him because they both liked talking. I love looking at people's gardens and Terry said, 'Right we'll have a walk round then'. It's absolutely beautiful and you can see Windsor Castle in the distance. I said, 'Years ago, did you ever dream about having a place like this?' and Terry said, 'Well you don't, do you?' I quoted that line from the song in *The Sound of Music* 'Somewhere in your youth and childhood you must have done something good' and I think he was a little moved.

When Ray was doing the voice overs on 'Come Dancing' Terry was doing the in-vision. And when they did the Variety Club awards Ray would always be the one outside tied to the railings with the wind blowing his hair. Then he'd say, 'Now over to Terry Wogan,' and Terry would be immaculate inside. When we were doing an outside broadcast of 'Come Dancing' we'd all be in our glad rags and afterwards if it was summer, we'd stroll down the street, have a drink in a bar and then perhaps go out to supper. But Terry by this time was very well known and he'd go straight back to his hotel in a cab. Ray said, 'I'd never want to be in the position where I can't stroll down the street.'

Drink never affected Ray's work but when he wasn't working he would sometimes get terribly drunk. Certainly, as soon as he got some money in his pocket as a young man he spent it on drink. He loved to get in a pub with the rest of the guys and if he just had a few drinks he'd be great, perhaps get a bit silly but very funny. If he had too many however he used to go into himself, become very quiet and brooding. The next day he'd be so sorry, full of remorse. He was these two people, because though he was confident in his work, he was never totally confident about himself. Most of the time at parties he'd just have enough. But certainly there were times when I could see that he was going to have too much. He'd do it usually when he was worried about something. He'd use drink to anaesthetise himself instead of talking about what was tormenting him.

After a particularly bad night I'd say, 'Why do you do it Ray?' and he'd say, 'I don't know'. There were some bad patches that were so black I used to think, 'Whatever is going to happen?' Sometimes when he'd had an awful lot of wine to drink it used to get me annoyed. One evening I said, 'Ray, I can't go on with you behaving like this. When you're so awful I think of leaving you,' and he said, 'Okay, why don't you go?'

I didn't sleep at all that night, I was so upset. I kept thinking 'Perhaps that's what he really feels deep down and he really does want me to go.' Next morning I said, 'Ray do you remember our conversation last night?' He said, 'A bit of it. What did I say?' I needed to know the truth and I told him what he'd said. I asked him if he really wanted me to go out of his life and he was absolutely appalled and apologetic and loving. He kept saying 'Alma, I'm sorry, I didn't mean it, I love you so much.' This kind of thing only happened occasionally but it was always awful when it did.

I did have certain feelings of insecurity and jealousy particularly in the early period. It disappeared for a while when we were happy together, but then in the later years it came back. I was obviously getting older and Ray was reaching his peak. He and his producer Denis O'Keeffe went to Sweden to do an interview with Abba; Ray adored Abba. When he came back he was telling me that Stig Anderson, their manager, had an island with the most wonderful house and he'd invited them all over one evening. Pierre Salinger had also been there and Ray said, 'I fell in love with Agnetha Faltskog, she's so beautiful'. I said, 'You didn't did you?' and I felt a real spark of jealousy.

Sometimes I'd hear him introducing one of Abba's records and he'd often say, 'Agnetha makes my toes curl,' and I used to feel upset again.

I'd think, 'He does mix with all these glamorous people. I wonder if he ever meets a girl that he really fancies?' Ray was very aware that I was extremely conscious of the fact that I was nine years older than him and he was brilliant at reassuring me. He could make me feel okay both with words and with action. He used to say, 'Who do I come home to? Who do I want to come home to?' He could be very jealous as well and he was always worried that I'd meet some rich silver-haired business man.

We did have a very difficult period when I started going through the menopause because I went off making love for a while. I'd had a hysterectomy which had given me a false menopause, then I had the real one and it played hell with my emotions and hormones. Ray was just at the peak of his manhood and he found he was living with a wife who was saying 'No, I don't want to' all the time. I think he was worried initially that I wasn't in love with him any more. He was a passionate man, a very caring lover and that was a difficult time. It was his life style that helped us through, because once he became a regular on the Radio 2 early morning show he was going to bed at 9.00. He'd have been up at 3.30 in the morning, probably worked all day and he'd be exhausted. We got into a pattern of life where we didn't make love so much but we always had what we used to call a 'cherish'. It started when we were living at The Priory and often in the afternoon, when Ray was doing shifts we'd go and lie down on the bed. He'd have his arm round me, my head would be on his shoulder and we'd have a kiss and a cuddle and a little snooze.

In many ways it was more meaningful than sex. Whenever he was away, doing an outside broadcast and I hadn't gone with him, he'd write letters and cards. Sometimes, he'd even send one from Heathrow before he flew out. He was working once in Monte Carlo and he sent me a little note saying, 'I love you with all my heart, I've missed you terribly this past week, it seems like a lifetime. Still, when the postman delivers this, we'll be chuckled up in bed together. Can't wait'.

One of the sad things when he became ill was that we couldn't make love any more, we couldn't even have a 'cherish'. I couldn't snuggle under his chin because of the dressing so I'd snuggle down and try and put my head on his chest, and then some times when we got into bed I'd link his arm but it was difficult. In the end I had the strength for the two of us but he was still worrying and thinking about me right till the end. He'd say, 'Alma, I've got to be close to this horrible thing on my neck but I don't want you getting too near it'. It was sad but there were so many other things that made up for that. We missed out on physical intimacy but emotionally we were even closer. We were more in tune than we'd ever been and that balanced the sadness out. It must happen to a lot of people, and that closeness mentally is something I treasure. We seemed to know what the other was thinking. It's amazing how things compensate.

[6]

We moved into our little cottage in Blackheath in October 1985 and Ray absolutely loved it. Later when he became ill I used to say to him, 'This is terrible Ray. We've saved money and you've worked so hard. It's not right, not fair. You've not had long enough, in this lovely little house.' He'd say, 'Well never mind, at least I have been able to live here and enjoy it'.

Every evening when we went to bed, he'd go to lock the front door and he'd walk down the path and lean on the gate, looking at the heath. Our bedroom was at the front of the house and as I was drawing the curtains I'd look out and see him. When he came up to bed, I'd say, 'I saw you,' and he'd say, 'Well it is great, isn't it?' Ray changed me totally because before I met him I tended to think of everything as black or white, right or wrong. I was a better person for knowing him. He taught me to look at any situation and try to see why people behaved as they did. He brought out a lot of good in me, he taught me not to be dogmatic. But neither of us were joiners. He never joined clubs. I like to do things on my own which is why I like jogging because I do it in my own time.

He believed that life was meant to be fun and he could always see the funny side of any situation. Sometimes he'd do some home decorating, he'd find himself at the top of the ladder painting the ceiling, with a knotted hanky on his head, and for some reason he thought this was an absurd thing for a grown man to be doing. He'd be laughing so much the tears would be pouring down his face. The ladder would be shaking and I'd be holding it saying, 'Ray be careful, you're going to fall off'.

The first hint I had that anything was wrong was when he was shaving one morning. I could see this little lump and I said, 'Ray what on earth is that?' I felt it and it was rock hard but he just said, 'Oh it's nothing, it will go away.' I said, 'You've got to go and see a doctor'. So in the end he agreed to make an appointment but he wouldn't let me go with him. His appointment was at 11.30 on September 3rd 1987 at the private London Bridge Hospital. At 12.30 he had to get on a train and go to Gateway Production Company for an hour's booking for a voice-over. He said, 'If you come with me, we'll both get upset and I won't be able to work'.

He hadn't been able to face the thought of waiting and queuing up which was why he was going as a private patient. I think, even then, we somehow knew it was something serious. He went along, asked a lot of questions and the doctor told him it was cancer of the mouth. He then said that Ray might be able to work for about six more months and that he probably had about two more years to live. I just find it unbelievable when I look back at Ray's sheer bloody courage. He came out of the hospital, had a pint in the nearest pub and then he got on the tube and went to Gateway Productions to do his voice-over. Afterwards he came back to central London to do another voice-over for Colour Film Services. I'd been on an outing to Southend with a group of stroke patients from Greenwich Hospital and I didn't get home till after six. Ray was there when I got in and he had a very serious face. He said, 'It's the worst we could possibly have imagined. It's malignant'.

We both cried and cried that night and Ray drank a lot of red wine. We were terribly upset, weepy and tried to comfort each other. I wasn't really surprised because in my heart I'd known it was bad but I was bloody annoyed that the doctor had actually said two years. It would have been so much better if he'd said, 'Perhaps you haven't got a long time left,' because doctors shouldn't play

God. A lot of people would just curl up and die at the end of those two years. It's like putting a sentence of death on somebody. I said, 'Come on Ray, he doesn't know how strong you are'.

He was extremely upset when he talked about work. He said, 'Eventually, I'll have to stop broadcasting,' and that really broke him up. I was trying to be reassuring and my first reaction was 'We must get a second opinion'. However, I think deep down, Ray knew that the man was right. But the news was difficult to take on board because at this time Ray felt extremely well. We both just cried and cried for quite some time and it was important we did.

In the end we went to bed and just lay there with our arms around each other. I kept thinking, 'This can't be happening to Ray, my good, kind, lovely Ray'. The following day Ray had a booking in a big dance hall in Bridlington working with Joe Loss. Joe has a terrific following and the place was packed. He's a smashing chap and he and Ray always got on really well. This night he'd absolutely no idea that Ray was ill and he gave him the most generous introduction. He said, 'And here is the young man with the fabulous voice, who is going to be with us for years to come.' Ray was on stage listening to this and he then went on and did the most wonderful programme. I was just standing at the back digging my nails into my hands and thinking, 'Oh Joe, if only you knew'.

We did get a second opinion from the dental surgeon at University College Hospital which only confirmed what he had been told. We went on to find out everything we possibly could about this form of cancer. Ray kept saying, 'I've half an idea it just might go away as quickly as it came'. And I had to say, 'Hang on a minute Ray. You've seen the top guys, they wouldn't make a mistake'.

When he was younger he used to believe God would wreak hell and damnation on him and he did for a while feel that his illness was a repayment for his life. I could never see God doing that, and in truth it was a combination of many things – smoking, drinking and his life-style included which must have taken its toll. He worked incredible hours but he packed an awful lot into his forty-seven years. In fact it was his beloved work that helped him through the next few months. He found it easier to cope with the cancer when people still didn't know. But I found it harder. It was because he was still broadcasting that he thought it wasn't right to announce he was ill. He was convinced that it would have changed his relationship with the listeners.

The sensible side of me knew that if somebody is diagnosed as having terminal cancer, then they're not going to get better. But that meant there would be no Ray and I couldn't bear to come to terms with that. Every night, we'd have a little cry and then fall asleep in each other's arms. In the beginning, the cancer was still just a little lump. It was when it broke through the skin for the first time and started to bleed, that we began to realise what was really going to happen. We were still leading a normal life and Ray grew a beard to hide the lump. People would make jokes and ask him why he'd grown it. He'd give daft reasons and say, 'Oh I just fancied a change,' or 'I can't afford a razor blade'. It was a strange, mixed, emotional time. Sometimes I'd lose my temper over daft little things and then immediately I'd hold him tight and say, 'Oh love, I didn't mean that'. Ray never got annoyed but I was sharper more quickly than I would have been in normal times because of the tension.

The first people we told were David and Julie. We went to Paul's christening in Salford in September and Ray said, 'It's going to be a lovely, happy day, we mustn't spoil it. They're going off on holiday soon. We'll tell them when they get back.' We were staying at the Midland Hotel in Manchester because we felt then we'd be able to escape if we needed to. The hotel had just been completely revamped and we said to David and Julie that we'd like to try it out. We all had a meal together on the Friday. Ray was wearing his red velvet jacket and we tried to be normal but I don't think we really carried it off. They're very observant and David said later, 'There was something in both your eyes'. He and Julie thought there might be something wrong between Ray and me, though they couldn't really believe it. The christening was a beautiful sunny day, everybody was drinking champagne in the garden. I thought we were being our usual selves, but Julie said, 'Is anything wrong Alma?' I said, 'There is something wrong but I don't want to upset the party, I'll tell you some other time'.

We got back to the hotel, the phone rang and it was David. He said, 'Look Mum, there's no way we can go on holiday not knowing what's wrong. Whatever it is, maybe we can help'. I just burst into tears and David says now that what went through his head immediately was that maybe Ray had cirrhosis of the liver. Ray came to the phone then and he just told David quite factually and calmly. He said, 'You've probably realised already that something is wrong. I've got a malignant tumour, they don't expect me to live longer than two years.' Julie was listening by the phone and Ray just told them all the facts. Their worst fears were realised, but it was better that they knew because otherwise there would have been barriers between us and there had never been barriers. The four of us had always been able to talk about anything, to cry in front of each other. I think at that moment Ray was just heartbroken for David and Julie because he loved them so much and he knew that they loved him. I certainly knew there was no way that I could tell my mother so I said to David, 'At some point when you think it's right, tell Gran'.

When we got home, I said, 'Ray, don't you think you ought to let somebody at the BBC know. Suppose you just keeled over one day in the studio?' In the end he told Frances Line, head of Radio 2 and he did it against his better judgement. He said, 'Please don't tell anybody else,' but she did in fact tell David Hatch. We also knew we would have to tell Ray's mother, before anything appeared in the press. We went up to Liverpool soon after that and Ray stopped off and got a bottle of champagne at the off-licence as he always did. We were just chatting about various things, drinking our champagne and then I heard Ray say, 'We're here because we've got something to tell you'. He was very calm. He just told his Mum and Jan that he'd found this little nodule in his neck and that he'd been to see the specialist who had said it was a malignant growth. We all had a lot of tears and his mother said, 'How long have you got to live?' He said, 'At the most two years'. She was very, very upset but she is a trained nurse and she then went on to ask some very practical, sensible questions about the progression of the cancer.

Ray kept saying to me, 'When do you think I'll know that I have to come off air?' and I'd say, 'You'll know, Ray'. It was becoming a real effort for him to enunciate properly and the strain on him every morning must have been terrible. He was not only having to think what to say, but to concentrate on controlling his tongue. Every morning, when he'd finished the programme, all the muscles around his mouth were aching with the effort he was having to make. He was also by this time, having to wear a small dressing on his neck. People would ask him what it was and he'd say it was an abscess. One day he had a haemorhage in the studio which wasn't very funny. He no longer had any saliva in his mouth and also his bottom teeth were loosening up. The family of a listener called Alice Arrowsmith had written in asking him to give her a dedication and on the morning of Thursday January 28th he tried to do it. He just couldn't force his tongue round the words properly and he knew it didn't sound good. When he came off air he listened to the tape and he said to Denis O'Keeffe, 'I think this week had better be my last'. All along I'd said, 'It's better to come off while you're still feeling good, rather than dribble on'. He'd kept asking and asking me what I thought. He needed a lot of reassurance though usually when it came to his work he was very clearsighted.

Denis O'Keeffe told Frances Line that Ray would do his last programme on the following day but she told him that she didn't want Ray to come in. She said, 'We can't expect him to do a final progamme and say goodbye, it would be too much'. Ray was devastated when he was told that he wasn't to do the Friday slot, that his broadcasting career that he'd loved so much was all over. He thought it was awful not going in and finishing the week off. I tried to comfort him by saying, 'Remember how emotional you get, even when you're just going away for a couple of weeks holiday'. He'd be in tears. If he'd done that last show he'd have been there, knowing it was the last day he would ever broadcast in his life. He'd also be having to make a huge effort to make his mouth work. I can see why Frances made that decision, but if she had let Ray do that one final show, I'm sure he would have done it and done it well.

Frances is a difficult lady to get to know. She writes wonderful letters but in a social situation it's impossible to have a conversation with her.

On the Friday morning Ray woke at 3.15 am as he did every morning when he was doing the show. He was a bit tearful, but then he actually did manage to have another sleep. We'd been told that the BBC were going to put out a press statement on the Friday and Bryant Marriott, the Controller, rang up and read it over to Ray on the telephone. We had a few phone calls from reporters, some came to the door. One photographer came round and wanted to take a picture and we said, 'Oh all right then'. On the Saturday we were going into the village shopping and on the billboards were headlines saying 'Tragic DJ'. It was unbelievable, it seemed as though it was happening to somebody else.

We got so many wonderful letters and cards the next few days and in the end the BBC just used to send them round in sacks. It was an outpouring of love and grief and it overwhelmed us for a while. You could just feel this huge support of powerful emotion. In some ways it was almost too much for Ray to bear but he loved the funny letters. There was a lovely one from cartoonist Bill Tidy who wrote: 'My lovable Italian wife Rosa pointed out your picture in the press to me today. "Hey" she said "thatta nice man who presenta Itsa Knockout . . ." So you see, nothing is in vain, and all those years of toil and struggle eventually got you mixed up with men dressed up as spring onions and girls in wet Tee shirts representing New Brighton'.

Terry of course wrote several times while Ray was ill and he used to ring up. In one letter he said, 'Dear old Ray, Hope this finds you sitting up on the plumped pillow, taking nourishment. I believe a coddled egg, beaten up in a pint of porter, is a sovereign remedy for what ails you. Too much snout and scouse, that's been your downfall; a healthier diet is indicated, with the emphasis on fried bread, chips and strong tea with sugar. My grandmother used to chew seaweed. She died young. Is Alma still on the chewing baccy? You have to admire her persistence. I just wish her aim was better, at the spittoon. She *ruined* my favourite snakeskin loafers, you know. I understand you've given up the fags and taken to the Meerschaum. Sensible laddie – you'll not be pestered with visitors, and even those who do brave the smog won't be able to find you. Heavens, but I miss your croaking of a morning – do you realise you were the only thing between me and the booby hatch for years? Me and a few million others. Shake off this foul ague and get behind that microphone again. The country needs you. And while you're up, we'll go out for a pie and a pint with your man Sinatra. It'll keep him off your back . . .'

Just after Ray came off air we got a brochure through the post with pictures of villas in Portugal. I said to Ray, 'I know who sent this'. I rang David and Julie and said, 'Thank you for the brochure'. They said, 'We've picked out a lovely villa, what about you and Ray coming with us?' Ray said, 'It's a smashing idea but it's in May and I just don't know how I'll be by then.' I said, 'Let's book it. It will be something lovely to look forward to. It's a villa, which means there won't be any other guests so you can lie in bed for as long as you want to. And if we have to cancel it when the time comes, well it's only money'.

Ray agreed and in the end we had a lovely time. He did a lot of walking. He couldn't swim, but he paddled and he got very brown. The villa was on a hill and he insisted on pushing the baby's trolley but he used to get very breathless. Paul had just learnt to walk, he was staggering about holding the furniture and going off into peals of laughter. Ray used to play games with him and they'd count shells together on the beach. It really was as though the child knew he had to be special to Ray. Julie and David just treat Paul like a little adult and he never screams or cries. He calls me Amo because I didn't want to be just another grandma. He's got so many and I didn't want to get lost in the crowd. The villa was beautiful, with its own little pool and lovely views. David and I used to get up early and go to the local market to buy fresh fish, which we'd barbecue in the evenings. By this time I was doing the dressing for Ray and he was extremely frightened, not about dying, but about the illness and the way he might die.

He always assured me that death held no fears for him and the talks he had with Harry Read, his friend from the Salvation Army, reassured and strengthened him. Ray believed there is life hereafter. He used to say, 'When somebody like my Dad dies, they can't just become nothing. All that vibrant strength and happiness can't merely vanish.' I'm certainly convinced that he was right, that Ray is still around and I look forward to meeting him again. This is just a little gap in our lives.

* * *

The holiday really was therapeutic and afterwards Ray wrote a little letter to Paul saying, 'Dear Paul, us two poor old trouts would like to thank you very much, for a lovely holiday at the sea side. We really enjoyed ourselves, although on balance I think we could have done with a bit more fish. I'm sorry if sometimes I was a little less than the life and soul of the party but that's just Because. Anyway, you more than made up for it, with all your wonderful games like pouring orange juice down your trousers, biting Mummy, tossing your balls in the water and poking shells through the French windows. Managing to eat most of my meals for me was an act of great friendship and very much appreciated. Sadly I had to drink all the wine myself. To see your smiley, sunshiney face every morning was the best tonic I could wish for and revived the flagging spirits of a raddled old man. Tell you what, ask your Mum and Dad to fetch you down here for a week or so real soon . . . You are all such dear kind people and we love you to dollrags'.

Later that year doctors at University College Hospital started Ray on a course of chemotherapy, and then they suddenly stopped it after he had had only three sessions, without telling us. When you're having chemotherapy, you have to ring on the morning of the day you're due to go in, just to confirm things. When I rang this particular morning the receptionist said, 'Oh, Mr Moore's treatment has been cancelled'. I said, 'Well that's the first I knew of it.' I rang the doctor's office and I managed to get through to the consultant. I said to him, 'I'd like to know why the treatment has been cancelled?' He said, 'What's the point of carrying on with expensive treatment, when it's doing no good.' I said, 'How do you know?' He said, 'We can tell'.

In fact both Ray and I remembered that before he'd started the course he was told that it wouldn't be possible to know the effect it had had until the end but they denied saying that. I said, 'Nobody told us. We're up and ready to leave for the hospital, hoping and thinking perhaps the chemotherapy is helping. And then we suddenly find out that somebody has just decided to stop the treatment, halfway through.'

I was so angry, because anybody dealing with terminal cancer patients should surely deal with them in a caring way. And I felt sure that if this kind of arbitrary treatment was happening to us, it was damned well happening to other people. I said to Ray, 'We're not going back there,' and Ray said, 'You're dead right babe, we're not,' because we could still laugh. It was early September 1988 that the treatment was cancelled and the doctor said, 'I think you ought to come in and talk about it'. Ray went to see him on September 15th but he wouldn't let me go with him because he knew I'd have laid into the consultant. He just told Ray that the treatment wasn't doing any good, but I think the way the whole thing was handled was appalling.

Often a cancer patient is depressed and low. If you say, 'What's the matter?' they may well say, 'I'm frightened to death.' The normal automatic reaction then, is to try and rally them round, to say, 'Come on cheer up, things aren't so bad.' But this is wrong, because what you are doing is repressing their feelings, implying they shouldn't be feeling depressed. Instead you should sit down, put you arms round them and say, 'I know. It must be terrible. Do you want to talk about it?' They might not want to discuss it at that moment but at least you've opened the way.

Whilst Ray was ill, Harry Read wrote a special prayer for us which ended, 'Let Ray and Alma place their hands in Thine. And let Thy peace their loving hearts entwine'. Ray and I always felt we were leaning on Harry and Win, his wife, but then Harry said that they've learnt things from us. I always thank Harry and Win for the love and support they've given me and since meeting them I've learnt to pray at any time of day. If I'm walking across the heath to the hospital and the sun is shining then that's a wonderful time. I pray for guidance and the strength to follow it. And basically I say thanks for everything, the good times and the bad, because Ray always believed that you gained from both.

Ray died about 6.20 on Wednesday January 11th 1989. Harry Read had been with him earlier in the day and when he heard the news he and Wyn came straight back. I left them with Ray so they could say their goodbyes to him and then Harry came into the kitchen. He said a little prayer with us all and it did help. In the evening we were all tearful but we felt good. We were talking about the daft things we'd all done over the years with Ray and about the stories his Dad used to tell when he was alive. It was a happy feeeling because we were remembering happy times. We were just so thrilled that Ray had been released. We were really on a high and that was before we'd had a drink. I was also very aware that if I started crying and being miserable then everybody else would have done the same thing. I didn't want that and I didn't see what good it would have done. Ray kept saying to me before he died, 'You've got to deal with this thing in a good way'. I felt I had to set the mood, and in the end, the way I did it seemed to be okay for everybody including Ray's Mum. We opened the champagne and then later we sent the lads out for fish and chips because that's what Ray would have enjoyed.

When Ray and I first came to London I used to meet him at Broadcasting House when he was working late. We'd have a drink in the BBC Club, and then often we'd catch the train to Lewisham and go by bus from there to Blackheath. There was a fish and chip shop just by the bus stop, and we'd buy some and stand on the pavement eating them. I used to say, 'I wish your listeners could see the BBC announcer now, eating fish and chips at the bus stop'.

Above: On a promotion trip for British Rail, Chester, 1988

Right: Julie Pearce and Ray, 1986

Below: Walking the London Marathon course. Julie Mather, Alma, Julie Pearce and Maureen Trewhitt. Ray and David did it too

Above: An early morning live interview with Eddie Large during Cowes Week, 1987

Left: Ray, Denis O'Keeffe and the legendary Johnny Roadhouse on a Bog-Eyed Jog in Manchester

Below: Ray bumped in to Syd Little and his wife on the High Street, Cowes Week, 1987

Above: At Manor House Hotel, Castle Combe, 1986

Right: Janet Moore, Mrs Moore and Mrs King (Alma's Mother)

Outside broadcast in Deptford, South London, with Wendy Richard

Ray with 'Management',
February 1988

Above: Ray, Alma and Paul, 1987

Left: Alma and Julie at Julie's Dad's wedding in 1986

Below: Julie, David and Ray registering for the 100–mile walk on Blackheath, 1986

The queue outside Sherratt & Hughes in Manchester during a signing session, September 1988

Ray signing his autobiography, with Alma and John Wilcox, the ex-BBC producer who gave Ray his first programme on the Light Programme – 'Pop North'

Left: Ray's last gig – switching on the Blackheath Village lights in the Three Tuns pub, Christmas 1988

Below: Noel Edmonds with Alma receiving an award given to Ray for his outstanding contribution to UK music radio by The Radio Academy, April 1989

Below: The Gold Badge of Merit Award presented by the British Academy of Songwriters, Composers and Authors. Ken Bruce accepted it on behalf of Ray in October 1988

GOLD BADGE
OF MERIT 1988

We've only recently got a local fish and chip shop in Blackheath because for a long time the council wouldn't allow it. We had an Indian take-away, Chinese, pizzas, but fish and chips weren't thought posh enough for Blackheath.

When we'd finished the champagne we went on to the brandy. David had given me a very special, expensive bottle for a Christmas present which I was cherishing. Don, Ray's brother, had spotted it and brought it out and then when that was finished we started on what Ray used to call the cooking brandy. We always kept it in the kitchen and we'd have some with lemon and honey if ever we had a cold. In the early hours of the morning David and I kipped down with some pillows and blankets on the sitting room floor. We'd all done such a lot of talking about Ray and reminiscing that I just went to sleep straight away. I knew there was a lot that needed to be done the following day but something just seems to take you over and help you cope.

I felt very strong, as though I was being carried along, I had a powerful sense of being cared for. Next morning I talked to the reporters who came to the house. Sandy Chalmers who is in charge of press relations for BBC Radio asked me if I wanted to do it and I said 'Yes'. I wanted to do it for Ray's sake and for all the listeners who'd been so marvellous. We really did feel a tidal wave of love coming from them and I felt I had a duty to let them know what had happened. I felt it was right to do it, that I was finishing things off for Ray. Before the press came, I thought about what advice Ray would have given me. He would have said, 'Treat it like work, sit down, calm yourself and then get on with it and do the best you can.'

[7]

The mini-car firm we'd always used in Blackheath took David to Lewisham to register Ray's death, and the driver said, 'Ray used to tell some terrible jokes in the mornings'. Afterwards they wouldn't charge us anything. They said, 'This is for Ray.' The love people felt for him just kept cropping up again and again. Even now, people write to me and say, 'We want you to know we haven't forgotten you'. They then go on to tell me about what's happening in their lives as though I were a member of their own family, because that's how they thought of Ray.

David saw to everything involving the funeral arrangements and he was terrific. I didn't have to ask him, he just did it. I know he would have done it for me anyway but he was doing it for Ray as well. He came back from seeing the undertaker and he didn't want to be all doomladen. He said, 'How do you think Ray would fancy pink satin?' and I said, 'Oh I can't see Ray in pink satin.' I said to Ray's Mum and Jan, his sister, that it would be better if they went home and then came back for the funeral. They were anxious about leaving me but I just wanted to be on my own for a while in our own little house. On the night he died I said, 'Right, I want Ray laid out here and he's staying here until he goes to the funeral.' I know David was worried about my initial reaction but he didn't say anything.

I then went up stairs to see Ray. I walked into the room, I looked around and I could feel he wasn't there. It was just Ray's body lying on the bed, he'd gone and I felt good at that moment. I said to David, 'It's all right. They can take Ray's body now.' I know that a lot of people won't let the body leave the house but they're trying to hold on to something that isn't there.

Before the funeral our local bobby came round and said, 'There are one or two things we've got to sort out because of the crowds and traffic control. Do you want the funeral cortège to go the long, right way round the one way system or the wrong, short way down the one way system?' I just couldn't believe what I was hearing because it sounded so funny. I said, 'Oh Ray would adore this. And there's absolutely no question what he'd choose. He'd definitely want to go the wrong way down the one way system.'

The day of the funeral I felt I had a job of work to do. I made up my mind I was going to do it the best I could, which was Ray's training. He'd been through some terrible times personally, but he'd gone on and done wonderful programmes. I prayed for strength and I said, 'Come on Ray, you've got to look after me.' The only time I wept on that day was when all the family flowers arrived at the house and we laid them out in our little front garden. It was a beautiful morning and the garden was just a carpet of flowers with the sun shining on them. Julie and I both cried because suddenly it wasn't a job any more, it was just heartache and crying from your heart. Julie and I sat in Ray's study and wrote our messages on the cards.

Julie had got a little card with a sleeping baby on it that she'd bought to send from baby Paul with a red rose. She wrote: 'To dear Grumps. We spent only a short time together, but wasn't it great? You will always be in my heart and in my soul and your influence on my life will remain forever. All my love, Paul'.

I'd ordered a spray of flowers for Ray from me, because after the funeral I wanted the flowers to go to hospital for the patients to enjoy. You can't send wreaths to hospital or the patients think, 'What are they trying to tell me?' On the card I wrote the words of the song that I had written all those years ago. 'Well, I know some day, this precious dream will have to end. But I want you to know it was oh so very good my friend. And though the magic may all fade away, we will live and and love today, for tomorrow – who knows?' I wrote the words when I was travelling up to Manchester to see David as a little boy. The night before, Ray and I had been talking about our lives and how happy we were at that moment and wondering what was going to happen in the future. The train set off from Euston, I'd got a bit of paper and a pen in my handbag and I just scribbled down the words. They literally poured out of my head and when Ray died they seemed prophetic.

Ray once bought an electric blue jacket that he wore with black slacks and he loved that jacket. When I had to make the decision about what Ray should wear in his coffin I said to the undertaker, 'I don't want Ray in a shroud'. I can remember seeing my Dad in his coffin. I looked at him and I thought, 'Here's an ordinary working man, his hands all gnarled. He's in a white silk shroud and that's not my Dad.' I didn't like it and I thought, 'No way is Ray going to be in a shroud. If he's going to go, he's going how he'd like to be. I got out his clean underwear, socks, shoes, his slacks and his lovely electric blue jacket. And that's what he was buried in. I didn't really want to go to the undertakers to see him so David and Julie said they would go.

In all the hoo-hah, we'd forgotten Julie a little bit. She loved Ray, she used to write him wonderful letters but she hadn't been with us when he died and she said that she would like to see him and say goodbye. She was a bit worried before she went, but she came back and she said, 'He looked smashing Alma, I was able to say goodbye to him.' She wasn't frightened at all and I think Ray must have been hovering around saying, 'Don't worry Julie, it's all right'.

It might sound odd but I looked forward to the funeral

knowing that I'd be supported by wonderful friends who loved Ray so much. Ray had said to me, 'I don't want everybody miserable and weeping at my funeral'. I used to say to him, 'But we'll be upset Ray,' and he said, 'Just look at all the good times we've had. Make it into a celebration. If you start it off by being upbeat, then everybody else will follow suit'. I said, 'Right, I'll do my best'. I chose some great hymns including 'Veni, veni Emmanuel' which was his favourite. I thought, 'I don't want to be all in black, Ray didn't want that'. In the end I wore a white jacket over a black dress that Ray had bought me years ago. He'd just gone freelance, and we were walking back from Broadcasting House to Charing Cross. I spotted this black, crêpe dress in a boutique. I said, 'That's the ultimate little black dress,' and he said, 'Let's go in and you can try it on.' We still weren't quite sure about money because we didn't know how much work Ray would get, but I went and tried it on and it was stunning. When I was a kid going to the pictures, I loved the dresses that Vera Ellen used to wear when she was doing a dance number. They were always fitted to the waist and then the skirt would swirl out and around as she danced and this dress was just like that. Ray said, 'You've got to have it'. It cost £50, which was an awful lot of money in 1975 but I always loved that dress.

Just before the funeral I thought, 'That's the first posh frock Ray ever bought for me, that's what I'll wear.' I wore some cream boots I've had for yonks and the wool jacket and I felt just right. It's actually the sort of thing you could wear for a wedding. I can understand the reasons people wear black at funerals, but if you've got a church full of darkness it encourages you to feel miserable. Ray had said to me, 'I've had a wonderful life and I want you all to remember that'.

On the morning of the funeral, I got out of bed, opened the curtains and a bloke who'd just got out of a van was putting cones out, to stop people parking. We set off for the church going the wrong way down the one way system. The police held up the traffic and as the cars came down the one way system, I saw an old fashioned Unwins wine van draw up and stop at the junction. The man who was driving got out and stood to attention. He didn't have a hat but if he had he'd have doffed it, and it seemed so appropriate that it should be a van carrying wine. As we went through Blackheath all the shopkeepers had come to stand on the pavement, there was Reg the fish and all his staff in their long white pinnies, everybody from the butchers and people had come out of the Railway Tavern pub. Ray would have loved the whole thing and he'd have laughed so much because he found laughter in everything. I kept thinking, 'Am I doing all right, Ray?'

After the service we went to the Bardon Lodge hotel in Blackheath which Ray and I used to go to a lot. I'd arranged that there should be lots of wine with the buffet but a lot of people didn't realise that and they kept going to the bar to buy drinks. When I got the bill, the manager said, 'We won't charge you for the wine with the buffet because Ray's friends really enjoyed the bar. And they're certainly all very good spenders'. At the end of the day, there was a little coterie of hardened drinkers. David and Julie, Adrian John and his wife, Martin Connor of the Carrot Crunchers were part of the nucleus of the late stayers of whom Ray was always one. David said, 'Mum do you fancy some champagne?' and I said, 'That sounds lovely.' David got a bottle, then Adrian John ordered another and soon everybody was ordering it. David said, 'Can't you just see the headlines in tomorrow's papers? "Drunken widow downs eighteen bottles of champagne with her son whom she left as a child".' We kept inventing more and more lurid headlines and saying, 'Ray, you'd love this.' At some point I said, 'I think we really ought to eat.' So I asked the manager of the Bardon Lodge to book us a table for ten at the Laughing Buddha in Blackheath. We fell out of there at about midnight and I thought, 'It's been nice, a very good day.' I'll never look back on Ray's funeral as a particularly sad occasion. He'd have loved it, all his friends telling stories about him. It was a very happy funeral. I looked on it as Ray's day. Everybody was there because they wanted to be. Ray had a great ability for making friends.

The next day David and Julie went home and I spent the following fortnight replying to all the letters. I did one hundred replies each day. On the Friday after Ray's funeral, it was the second anniversary of Terry Waite's disappearance. There was a service for him at All Saints because he lived in Blackheath and that's where he worshipped. I went into the church for the service and all Ray's flowers were still there and I found comfort in that.

When Ray died the BBC decided that he shoud have a memorial service which would be broadcast live at 1.00 pm on Friday March 3rd. Sir Roger Cary is the man who always arranges the memorial services for the BBC. He'd organised those for Huw Wheldon and Russell Harty but I don't think he'd ever heard of Ray. I went to have lunch with him, Bryant Marriott, Sandy Chalmers and David Winter who was head of Religious Broadcasting Radio, to discuss the arrangements initially. We had lunch at the Gay Hussar in a private little room upstairs and Sir Roger had brought along a list of high-powered religious music. I thought to myself, 'It isn't what Ray would have wanted at all.' Bryant, bless him, said, 'This is to be a celebration of Ray's life, Alma. We can put anything in it that you choose.' I said, 'I'd like to think about it' and when I got home, once again, I did it like work. I took Ray's stop watch out, got out all his favourite singles, listened to them and as I was listening the tears just flooded down my face. Then I picked out his favourite tracks from the LPs and played those. The minute I got to Sinatra singing 'It was a very good year' I thought, 'That's got to be in somewhere,' because the words were just like Ray's life. I listened to *Little Night Music* and *Chorus Line* and then the very last one I came to was *La Cage Aux Folles* which he adored.

I played, 'The best of times is now', timed it and I thought 'There can be no other choice'. Ray loved the words, he used to turn up the volume when he played it so it belted out and the song was so true for us. We always were conscious of how good things were and we never took anything for granted. After the memorial service I got a lovely note from Jerry Herman who wrote that song, saying how privileged he felt that it had been used. Ray would have been so thrilled to know that.

Harry Read read the lesson and did a personal little bit to Ray from his heart and Colin Berry gave the first address about Ray and the times they'd shared. I'd said to the producer that I'd love Terry Wogan to be involved and Terry came back especially early from his holiday, to give the second address. On the day of the memorial service at All Souls, Langham Place, David and Julie and I went over about 11.00, just to say hello to the people who were rehearsing. The Salvation Army band were there and the Syd Lawrence Orchestra were playing some of Ray's favourite tunes and I had a couple of tears. We then went to the St George's Hotel where Ray used to hold his champagne breakfasts. We'd said to the family and a few friends that that's where we'd be if they wanted to join us and quite a few of them did.

We had coffee and sandwiches and then the champagne started arriving and Spike Mullins the comedy script writer said, 'This is the way to do it'. The whole thing took off and we had a really lovely little time. I just hadn't wanted to go to the service straight from home. I said to Peter Donaldson the Radio 4 announcer, 'This is Ray's last gig, so it's got to be good.'

When it was time to go over to the church we came out and there were crowds of people and all the press. I thought, 'Ray would kill himself laughing if he could see this.' People had come a very long way just to be there. There were listeners from Scotland, from the North of England. Family, friends and colleagues were on the ground floor, listeners who'd written in for tickets were upstairs. So many people turned up without tickets, that they were allowed in the crypt where they watched everything on a video so nobody was left out. When we went into church, there was a single red rose lying on my seat. Evidently one of Ray's listeners had brought it. She'd said, 'I know Ray would want Alma to have this'. I still don't know who she was but the strange thing is that a few days beforehand, Betty Shine, the medium and author, had rung me up. She said, that Ray had been through to her and said he wanted me to have red roses on the day of the memorial service. Betty also gave me some red roses and when I told her what had happened she said, 'Ray's working through two of us now'.

The concert and the service were such a triumph, really exciting. The only time I had a tear was when Syd Lawrence's trombonist was playing 'Here, there and everywhere'. It's the song that Ray used to use as his signature tune when he did his series 'Ray Moore's Saturday Night' in the 'seventies. Sometimes the programme would be broadcast from a dance hall or a night club but other times he'd do it from the studio. He invented a mythical nightclub called Chez Ray. He convinced people that he was in this lovely night club with a girl singer sitting next to him. All the time of course he was just in his little studio. He'd say 'Come on, cuddle up closer'. He'd create this intimate atmosphere, play a schmaltzy record and people really believed it existed.

It was wonderful watching the Salvation Army band with their faces shining and when they did 'The Best of Times is Now' with the Syd Lawrence Orchestra, the choir and everyone on stage, it was just electric.

I never thought I'd see a hard nut like Syd Lawrence get so carried away and then when there were shouts for an encore, I thought how awful to have an encore in church. But then I said to myself, 'No, it's not. Because that was Ray. He never wanted things to end'. A lot of people that day said they felt he was sitting up on stage with the band.

I wore a trouser suit that Ray had bought me in Llandudno when we'd had a weekend there with David and Julie and Paul just after Ray had come off air. We were walking past this superb little boutique and I saw this lovely trouser suit. I said, 'Oh Ray that's fantastic,' and he said, 'That would be lovely on you, Alma'. I said, 'Oh no, it will be terribly expensive.' Later he said, 'Let's go and get that trouser suit for you. What are we saving up for, Alma?'

He loved buying me clothes and I think his Mum used to think I was extravagant but I like to buy really good things. I look after my clothes very well and I know they'll last. We went back to the shop, I tried it on and Ray said, 'That looks good on you, let's get it.' It's Italian in dark grey with a white overcheck. It has a straight little jacket and Ray said, it was like the old Beatles jackets. It was the last outfit Ray bought me so I thought that's what I would wear.

The programme was broadcast live at a time when David Jacobs should have been doing his show. He said, 'I'm so pleased, Alma because it means I can be here'. Ray used to pull his leg on air, say all sorts of daft things about him. When Ray was ill David wrote and rang several times. He's such a kind man.

After the service, we went back to the BBC for drinks and a

buffet lunch and then a lot of us went over to the Northumberland Arms. It's a pub that Radio 2 people use a lot. We stayed there for ages and then Adrian John said, 'We need something to eat. I'm taking you for a meal. I've booked a table in a Chinese restaurant that we go to quite a lot'. He and his wife Joy took David and Julie and me and the manager showed us downstairs.

We were having this lovely meal, talking about the service but there was nobody else in the room. I said to Adrian, 'It's a lovely place but it doesn't seem very busy.' When the waiter came over next time Adrian said, 'You're not doing very good business tonight.' He said, 'Mr John, we thought, tonight you'd like to be private.' Adrian had told them why he was booking a table so they'd kept everybody else out of that particular room. Afterwards Joy drove us all home because she doesn't drink. It really had been a superb day. I had a little word with Ray when I got into the house as I always do. I said, 'Well Ray, it was all absolutely smashing. I hope you enjoyed it'. I'm sure he'd adored everything.

After the memorial service I began to realise what it means being on my own. I began to cry a bit more thinking, 'What am I going to do without Ray?' I thought, 'I'll give myself a year before I make any big decisions'. I get asked to lots of things and sometimes I think in my low moments, that people are only asking me because I was married to Ray. But then I think, 'Well isn't it great that he matters so much? Ray used to be President of the League of Friends of the Gables, which is a home for mentally handicapped adults in Blackheath. After he died I got a letter from the Chairman Peter Moss asking me if I would take on the role in his place. I rang him and I said, 'I'd love to. Would you like to put Mrs Ray Moore on the notepaper?' He said, 'No. Because we want Alma Moore.' I was very touched by that.

A week after the memorial service I went on holiday with David, Julie and Paul. I was looking forward to being in a place where nobody knew Ray Moore or me. But it was a terrible realisation of how lonely it feels being in a hotel room on your own. It was great during the day, playing with Paul on the beach, but then after dinner, I'd say goodnight and then I'd walk back to this little empty room and I hated it.

The second week we drove to Key West and the agent had booked us into a terrible hotel with rooms overlooking the car park and the fish market. Julie said, 'I'm not bloody staying here.' It was on the main road, there was nowhere for Paul to play. David rang the travel representative in Miami and said, 'It said in the brochure that this was a family hotel which it certainly isn't.' She said, 'It's the only hotel where we have rooms in the area.' David said, 'Well we're going to check into the nicest hotel and we'll sue you when we get back home.' Julie and I were looking through the yellow pages at the time and we found one which looked nice. The rep said, 'Have you thought of another place?' so David mentioned the one we'd found. She said, 'It's very expensive' and David said, 'At this point I don't care. Book it.' The only accommodation they had vacant was the penthouse suite and that was wonderful. It was like staying in our own flat and I didn't have that awful sense of isolation. There was a jacuzzi, a beautiful sitting room, wonderful views over the sea and we had a super week.

Occasionally I'd go for a walk on my own and David and Julie understood. They were still grieving themselves because I wasn't the only one who had lost Ray. I don't think of myself now as a widow. I'm Ray's wife and he happens to have died. I force myself to do things but it feels particularly bad walking into a room where everybody is in pairs. I accepted an invitation to a

Radio 2 party where I thought I would know lots of people and there would be no problem. But it was difficult. At parties Ray and I would just mix around and Ray would keep saying, 'Alma, I want you to meet so and so'. I turned up at the party alone and intially it was all right because people came up to me. But every so often, I found myself standing on my own. I kept wishing that I hadn't come. Then I saw food was being served and I went and got some and joined the table where Colin Berry and some other people I knew were sitting. It was fine for a while but then once again I suddenly found I was the only one sitting there.

Mike Craig who is a producer at BBC North West in light entertainment came over, and he said, 'Darling how are you?' I said, 'Fine. But I feel a right nelly sitting here on my own'. He said, 'Why, what's the matter darling?' I said, 'Everybody's busy doing their own thing and I can't just mill about on my own.' He said, 'My darling, from now on you're with me,' and he took me around. He just behaved like Ray.

People say, 'Don't you find it difficult to sleep without Ray?' but I find it comforting being in our bed.

When Ray's first book was published he was asked to do another one and nearly until the end he worked on it every morning. He'd sit in his study writing and it meant so much to him. The words he wrote which are part of this particular book took a huge effort but I like to think that in a way they helped prolong his life.

Part two

RAY'S JOURNAL

While I was still on the air, I would never allow myself to believe just how popular and successful I had become. I would dismiss the fact that I was receiving over a hundred letters a day as an aberration; I used to tell myself that this would happen no matter who was doing the show. The fact that the vast majority of these letters were personal and highly flattering in an obtuse and po-faced sort of way, didn't sway me from this sort of total self-effacement. And when Gill Reynolds in the *Telegraph* referred to me as having a 'cult following', I feigned incomprehension. It was almost as if had I begun to seriously believe any of this, then I would no longer be able to perform the trick. Just as in a Tom and Jerry cartoon, when Tom is catapulted off the edge of the cliff, he can keep on running furiously through the air – only up to the point when he realises where he is and what he is doing. At that moment he drops like a stone. So I was often dismissive about myself, sometimes to the point of self-denigration.

I also never liked to analyse what I was doing on the air. Journalists asked me how I evolved my 'style', but I used to resist doing that, in case by capturing the genie, and subjecting it to scrutiny, it would suddenly evaporate.

Surely, Alma would say, the BBC wouldn't still want me to present a daily show on the national network if I was as mediocre as I claimed to be? I used to reply that probably the only reason they kept renewing the contract was that they couldn't find any other oaf who was prepared to get out of bed at 3.15 am, five days a week.

Of course, all of this was self-delusion. I now realise after six months away from radio and with letters, cards and phone calls still coming in, that I must have projected some powerful on-air persona to which people related strongly. I also realise – too late – that I must have been a very good broadcaster indeed to sustain two hours on the air every day, with no script, no guests, no quizzes, no 'spots' – just me in a curious dialogue with a vast unseen audience.

What they seemed to enjoy most of all was my sense of humour; I have never been any good at telling 'jokes', but in the early mornings they seemed to relish the whimsy and drollery that would evolve out of the music or the letters: I loved playing tricks with the conventions of radio itself – and when it all went well, the sense of exhilaration was almost tangible.

It may seem hard to believe that the start of each programme felt like the beginning of an exciting and dangerous adventure: it would be easy to assume that doing the show five days a week for all those years would bring on a kind of battle weariness, and a sort of mechanical factiousness. I never ever felt that each morning was new, each day was different. This is not the rosy spectacles of hindsight, but a feeling I vividly remember relishing each morning. That is why I continued as long as I could, I treasured and revered every moment.

The real thrill of the whole exercise for me, was that feeling of hang-gliding free-form through the airwaves, dotting on tip-toe from word to word, where logic and gravity were suspended. Coasting and soaring on thermal currents of quotes and phrases and technicolour pictures in sound. When it really worked well, it was a glorious feeling. The music and my words all melting into a ridiculously colourful kaleidoscope of sound. I make it all sound so pompous, but it was such tremendous fun.

Simple things seemed to fire the imagination of the audience:

I remember years ago, while wading through an interminable traffic bulletin, that I haphazardly referred to delays at Gatport Airwick. For some reason, this really got them going, until in the end I myself wasn't certain what the correct name for the wretched place was. As often happened, this then evolved into a saga about the windsock at Gatport Airwick, which elicited a response from Pat Houghton, who was evidently in charge of the Gatport Airwick windsock. As always with my audience, Pat fully entered into the whole arcane spirit of the thing by declaring that Gatport Airwick didn't just have one windsock – but three: one in the wash, one in the airing cupboard and one up the pole.

Pat's husband, Alan, then hove into view: he was evidently some kind of roving executive for British Caledonian, and began bombarding me with peculiar bulletins from Botswana, Namibia and a place I referred to as Zimbabweewee, whose President is a revered character by the name of Rev Canaan Banana. Alan would often forward fraternal greetings to me from the hallowed Banana. Thus, in the early twilight of those mornings, the surreal began to be the norm, and cold reality took on the air of the unusual.

After a week or two of this glorious nonsense, I got a letter from the Ambassador of Zimbabweewee, accusing me of racialism, being a lackey of the facist regime in South Africa, and denigrating the achievements of his magnificent People's Republic. The fact that the Rev Canaan Banana is to Western ears a funny name and Zimbabweewee is cheap play on the word, seemed to have eluded him. Irony is something people find difficult to recognise these days. And this whole palaver grew out of an inadvertent mispronunciation of an airwick – airport.

I think I probably made matters worse by pointing out that Mugabe backwards was E' ba gum! I still can't see quite what harm this would do to the great man in the corridors of power.

In fact, the travel news generally provided me with a plethora of hapless pitfalls. Being from Liverpool, I always had trouble with vowel sounds: it took a conscious effort to distinguish between 'fair' and 'fur', and 'spare' and 'spur'. My major problem arose at Heathrow where there was an Airport Spur, two words which interwove the problem. It often used to come out as Urport Spare, or Erpert Spur. In the end, perversely, I used to try and get it wrong, which in turn would evoke torrents of humorous derisive mail. The whole thing became a two way traffic, a strange conversation in which only one person was speaking.

Also arising out of the travel news were the wonderful sagas about abnormal loads, which in my fevered imagination quickly degenerated into abominable loads. I never had the remotest conception as to what these things could possibly be, but imagined them as enormous pre-historic behemoths of fiery temper who would lumber haphazardly along the highways and byways of Britain. The whole point of these bulletins was to warn motorists to avoid the route these things would be taking, but I used to enjoy colouring the reports by giving these abominable loads an independent perverse anthropomorphic existence.

It always appeared to me that they used to turn up in the oddest of places and then go mooching off to some equally improbable destination; one of these most favoured routes took them from Wisbech to Ottery St Mary. I would muse on the fact that the poor exhausted abominable load had hibernated for the winter in a copse in Wisbech, and had awoken in spring, scratched itself, rubbed its eyes and was suddenly taken with the notion of pushing off to Ottery St Mary. As it was on the road – nourishing itself on the top leaves of poplars and herbaceous borders – I used to enjoy warning motorists not to inflame the volatile passions of the creature, as they were overtaking. I especially liked telling them to avoid the temptation of pulling faces at it, or poking it in the belly with sharp sticks as this could lead to it becoming somewhat snappy, when it would likely sink its menacing molars into a wing mirror or radio aerial. To placate its mercurial disposition, I would advise drivers to toss it a chunk of Dundee cake as they went by – this of course had the effect of reducing the vast animal into a state of slobbering docility.

The whole thing was utter nonsense of course, but just as I enjoyed playing this silly game, so the radio audience too were captured by the sheer lunacy of the whole idea. And I am sure that by giving the travel news this arcane dimension, the information sank home far more effectively than if I had read it in a bald, flat-footed factual way.

Perhaps I was a little obsessed with animals because fictitious creatures also figured largely in the long-runing tarradiddle of Boggart Ol' Clough. Now this is the name of a real place just outside Manchester, and I gather that it's a sort of scruffy, wooded open space, much frequented by dog walkers and desperate star-crossed lovers. Quite how the whole palaver started remains a mystery, but I used to imagine that the boggarts were small furry, hobbit-like creatures who inhabited this Clough. Often in the very early mornings, it was easy to imagine small huddles of boggarts furtively making plans for the week-end, with their beady eyes surreptitiously eyeing the activities of the fearsome oo-floo birds, as they scavenged amongst the wild lupins. Other solitary boggarts would be up in the clutterbuck trees, solemnly nibbling nuts and berries, and little couples of boggarts would be sitting calmly at the side of their holes, studiously picking nits out of each others' ears. This idyllic bucolic scene would then be rudely interrupted by the sudden arrival across the brow of the hill of a half-crazed team of myopic middle-aged musicians, blowing a demonic threnody on an assortment of brass instruments and old ironmongery. At this point, I would then cue in a track from the Johnny Roadhouse Orchestra or some such. Rightly or wrongly, I felt that my pictures in words added greatly to the impact of what otherwise might have been a somewhat mediocre musical performance.

Written down in black and white like this, the whole thing seems childish in the extreme, and yet that early morning radio audience related very strongly to these colourful inventions. One lady in Essex wondered one morning if the Boggarts on the Clough were any relation to the legendary Waltons on the Naze.

* * *

I was always very conscious that I was working for the BBC, and not solely Radio 2. And so I began – as a kind of public service – to mention that if the listener didn't much care for my efforts on Radio 2, then there were three other BBC networks more than ready to cater for their tastes. In other words, don't switch to commercial radio, stick with the BBC – we have something for everyone. So I would cross-trail the 'Today' programme on Radio 4, hosted by the bewhiskered Brian Bed-stead, and recount tales of meeting him in the main reception of Broadcasting House at 4.30 am, where he would greet me with a cheery 'Morning, laddie – looking bloody rough again, eh?!' I used to idly wonder on the air why it took two presenting, a couple of dozen reporters, a newsreader, a weatherman and a god-bothering chap, to hold together a programme no longer than mine. Radio 4 was obviously some kind of job-creation scheme.

And then came Radio 1 with their morning show hosted by the talented Adrian John. For reasons which elude me still, Adrian wore sun glasses all the time; even at 4.30 on a January morning he would come breezing into the building in those ridiculous specs. I tackled him about it once and he seemed somewhat miffed: 'Not sunglasses, man; these are shades!' And so, poor boy, he instantly became Ade The Shades.

He was very much in tune with the sort of thing that would appeal to me, and would often tell me about some of the curious groups that would be gracing the Radio 1 airwaves through the day. They frequently had the most unbelievably inventive names, and I would implore my Radio 2 audience to switch to Radio 1 so that they could hear the likes of The Sensible Jerseys, A Guitar A Trumpet And A Drum Machine, Nine Out Of Ten Cats, One Of The Waiters, We're Ships At Sea – Not Ducks On A Pond, A Black Man A Black Man and Another Black Man, Silly Not To, and some lot called The The. Adrian once told me about a Maori group who were doing well in the Australian charts called Wanna-Wanna-Wee-Wee.

And I used to relish getting down to extolling the virtues of Radio 3, a network I love to listen to a lot, but which I felt needed a degree of debagging. Around the announcers' names and personalities, I used to like to weave a picture of an arcane team of grotesques: Malcolm Ruthven quickly became Talcum Malcolm, always smelling sweetly of California Poppy, and whose smiley polished apple face shone in the early daylight. The grizzled unkempt gruffness of Tom Crowe, whose main role in life was running a donkey sanctuary. The smooth and urbane Jon Curle, much given to sporting curious hats and cossack riding boots, and who I claimed – quite truthfully – lived in the same village as me, except that he was at the antiquarian bookshop end, and I was at the betting shop and launderette end. And then Elaine Padmore, otherwise the Radio 3 cleaning woman and a little treasure, Mrs Padmore, and who on Fridays would come in early and give the whole studio a burst of 'serious bottoming'. She was also the final arbiter as to exactly when the summer curtains had to be swapped for the winter curtains.

Poor Donald McLeod quickly degenerated into 'Old Muck-load'. The sepulchral voice of Peter Barker who would come and pinch my coffee, his white wiry hair standing on end as if he had been plugged into the mains all night. I used to reckon his hairdressers were Black and Decker.

And the delightful Patricia Hughes; gnarled old BBC hands were rumoured to address her as Pat, but to the rest of us, she was the redoubtable Miss Hughes, who ruled this team of recalcitrant announcers with an iron fist, while smelling sweetly of Chanel No 5. As well as a formidable presence, she also – between announcements – would attend to the needs of the studio in a lady-like way. Watering the rubber tree plant, dead heading the Busy Lizzies, and maybe sometimes a little light dusting. Her back y'know!

And finally the Head Boy and Senior Radio 3 pencil monitor – Cormac Rigby, often referred to lovingly as Tarmac Rigby; a man of small stature much given to scurrying about the studios with urgent bits of paper. He was invariably wearing a dark blue blazer with the BBC crest on the pocket, poking out of which were at least 47 pens of varying colours. He was considered by many of his cohorts to be a bit of a goody-goody and teacher's pet.

Frequently, I used to like to weave stories around this odd cast of characters: as when I said it was rumoured about Broadcasting House that Miss Hughes and Jon Curle were enjoying something of a clandestine liaison, and how they used to meet for breakfast in a little café with steamed-up windows just down the road. As the other diners attacked the mixed gorilla with a sort of nonchalant haste, Miss Hughes and Jon Curle would be holding hands under the table and making plans for the weekend.

All utter fiction, of course. But it did strike me as somewhat odd that most of the composers featured on Radio 3 were dead. Obviously it wasn't absolutely necessary to have shuffled off this mortal coil to get your stuff played, but it sure seemed to help. I also used to like mucking about with the composers names. Kodaly for instance, whom I used to insist was Australian, because he invented the well known phrase or saying 'G'day Kodaly'. And then there was the unspeakable Smetana. I used to like to imagine the whole studio littered with great steaming piles of Smetana under the desk, in the umbrella stand next to the rubber plant. Similarly, there was the equally noxious Poulenc, whose very presence would fill the whole studio with powerful noisome effluvia. If there was any Poulenc in the programme, Miss Hughes would carefully don elbow-length rubber gloves, and serve up the offensive Poulenc with surgical tweezers at arm's length. She was always meticulous in washing her hands thoroughly afterwards.

*   *   *

I have never written any of this down until now: when I was live on the air, I used to weave this whole ridiculous tapestry out of thin air, with only the name of the announcer on duty and the list of music he'd be playing as the raw material. Looking back now, the whole thing seems extraordinary: quite what a listener tuning in for the first time made of it all is anybody's guess, but by God, it was such tremendous fun for me.

*   *   *

In the middle of the 1980s, as Sinatra was coming up to his seventieth birthday, Denis O'Keeffe and I discussed seriously the possibility of doing an in-depth interview with the man to celebrate this auspicious occasion. It would, of course, involve a trip to Las Vegas or California. So we contacted Sinatra's fortress and were honoured with a reply from his attorney, who demanded to see a list of possible questions that I proposed asking. I forwarded an exhaustive list of some 200 questions, after which the trail went cold.

In fact, what I really wanted to do was to lean on a bar with Sinatra for a couple of hours with a tape recorder running, and just chat and reminisce about the Man and his Music.

Inevitably, I blurted out much of this saga on the air: it didn't seem a lot to ask really, to pop over to America, and buy Sinatra a pie and a pint in his local. After a Nancy Sinatra track, I would plead pathetically on the air for her to have a word with her Dad about me. Finally, in desperation, I came to the conclusion that perhaps Sinatra didn't fancy me cluttering up the bar in his local, so I hit on the brilliant idea of inviting him to mine. I had heard somewhere that he was often in London on private visits and so the short journey out to Blackheath would prove to be no problem. I felt sure that he would warm to the myriad charms of the Railway Tavern, with pints of bitter served in hot glasses, fistfuls of wet change and cold collations at the bar. All these inventive suggestions were greeted with a deafening silence, but perhaps my phone was out of order when he rang.

Again, the whole idea was a complete farce, but the audience responded in droves as to various other ruses and avenues I could explore to trap the great man. In the end all came to nought and I became a bit sniffy about the whole thing, and even stopped sending him birthday cards. By the way, I once thought I saw Sinatra on Platform 4 at Charing Cross station, but it probably wasn't him. If he didn't fancy Blackheath then I could hardly imagine him in East Croydon.

*   *   *

And Blackheath itself was fertile ground for some of my more whimsical ideas. It's the sort of place that imagines itself as having a somewhat higher station in life than is actually the case, the sort of neighbourhood where there are Mercedes parked outside the front doors, but inside the children are living on a diet of broken biscuits. 'All fur coat and no knickers' as my Dad used to say.

It's the sort of place where Michael Frayn and Glenda Jackson brush past sweaty men in bookmakers' suits in the village, the sort of men who have no visible means of support, but who, in the pub, pay for their drinks from great wads of oily tenners in their back pockets. And elegant, well dressed women who go in the butchers for 2 oz of scrag end of neck and pay by Access.

In Blackheath, no one goes out to work, they are all 'out at business'. In Blackheath there is no betting shop or chip shop, but we do have a turf accountant and a sea-food restaurant. At evening service at All Saints Church on the heath, there are often a stoic six souls in the congregation, but once when 'Songs of Praise' turned up, there was a fairly healthy stampede to get in, with mounted police keeping the crowds back outside.

It is a world in which Damon Runyon would feel very much at home. The elderly cockney couple well into their seventies, whose perverse delight is strolling around the village starting arguments. Then there's Society George, a tall lank individual of Irish origin and dressed in shiny demob suit, and who, after a couple of drinks will spontaneously treat passers-by to tearful Gaelic laments. The weather-beaten old gipsy woman who sits in the middle of the traffic island peeling carrots, and that middle-aged bod in the Railway Tavern who spends every lunchtime from 11.30 am till 3 pm wrestling breathlessly with the crossword in the *Sun*.

And the world of the pub also gave me great opportunities to take a gentle rise out of those lovable English conventions. In the Railway Tavern itself, there is a great tradition for the barmaid to take the glasses hot, straight from the dishwashing machine and immediately pull you a pint. There is something somewhat disappointing about sipping a delicious pint of beer out of a hot glass. And the inconsequential pub chat rather fascinates me.

'Pull up a bollard, old boy.'

'No, no. I'll get these in, I'm in the chair.'

And after two or three pints, the invariable, 'Have a drop of short, laddie!'

Even more inconsequential, 'I'll get these, I've got the right money.'

There's a chap who goes in the Railway and orders a Virgin Mary, which turned out to be Bloody Mary without any vodka. And the giggling girls from the bank who go in there and order halves of lager and blackcurrant. At Christmas time it becomes even worse when the once-a-year drinkers invade the place in force, and peculiar rounds of drinks keep being requested of the barman.

'One Bols, three egg-nogs, half a Guinness, a green chartreuse, four sweet sherries and two cider shandies.'

And when you've paid for the drinks, you invariably end up with a fistful of wet change.

I once knew an irascible barman at the BBC club at the Television Centre who flatly refused to serve anyone who wanted soft drinks or any sort of shandy.

And then there's the young chap who pokes his nose round the door of the Railway and shouts at the barman, 'Has he been in?' To which the answer is invariably, 'No, not this week, pal!'

This ridiculous pantomime is enacted about three times a week. I've never, in twenty years, discovered who the chap is looking for.

All of this silly material would be sprinkled daily in between the records at what seemed to me appropriate moments. But often I would launch into one of these fantasies as the whim took me, which I felt gave the whole show an even more surreal twist. I always wanted to surprise the listener, almost as if he would want to turn up the volume when I was speaking to see what the devil I would come out with next.

* * *

I used to enjoy those mornings, when at the end of a parliamentary session I would be coming across Westminster Bridge at 4.30 am and notice the lights still burning at the top of the Big Ben tower. This means that the political asylum is still hard at it. At the end of each term something called the Consolidated Fund Bill appears on the agenda, which is a convention by which any of the inmates who are still awake and/or sober, can raise any subject under the sun. I often used to like to muse on what sort of questions they would ask in this end of term atmosphere.

'Where is the Prime Minister going on her holidays?'

'Has she read any good books lately?'

'Can the Prime Minister tell the House, is Mickey Mouse a cat or a dog?'

But often the BBC itself gave me my richest vein of ore to mine; frequently these were serious groans, wrapped up in a thick veneer of heavy irony. Like the Budget programmes for instance. The Chancellor's speech normally starts at 3.30 pm when he proceeds to blather on at length about the green pound, the European currency snake, and bewildering sets of initials; ECUs, GNP, GDP, and this mysterious business about the M1 money supply. So it's often about quarter to five before the great man gets into the red meat of the thing with the taxes on drink and tobacco, which is the only thing anybody wants to know anyway.

But the BBC, for reasons only known to itself, always starts these Budget programmes at least half an hour before the

Chancellor has even entered the Chamber, which leads to the ridiculous spectacle of assorted studio-bound worthies and pundits, filling in time and playing that very popular media game, 'What if!'

'What if the Chancellor reduces beer to 6p a pint?'

'What if the Chancellor were drinking gin and tonic rather than Buxton water?'

'What if the Chancellor abolishes VAT on rowlocks and surgical boots?'

This crazy charade can be sustained for hours and frequently is. And then after the weary and tedium is beginning to fade away on great waves of national apathy, and when every last entrail of the Chancellor's words has been digested, the BBC thrusts on to the air a Budget Update, which regurgitates the whole palaver again. A whole new tribe of pundits is wheeled on to pontificate on the effects of the increase in beer prices on the Vietnamese boat people and how the rise in petrol taxes affects the average unborn child. Frequently we have to go to Taiwan, Kuala Lumpur and Tierra del Fuego for their reactions. All this can take us into the small hours of the morning.

In fact, the BBC has become obsessed with updates. The sleeping dog is never left to lie, and so we have 'Crimewatch Update', 'Olympic Update', 'Election Update' until the listeners' mind is so full of all these clothy words that the whole issue is a complete jumbled mass of meaningless issues.

*   *   *

I know nothing, and care even less about sport, and so I often used to like taking a gentle swipe at the BBC's fixation with it. In the early mornings there was always a two-minute sports bulletin which, of course, had to be filled come what may. So in the middle of February on, say, a Thursday morning when there would be absolutely nothing of sporting interest to report, they still had to find something to occupy the slot. This led them up into arcane blind alleys headlining the Regional Finals of the South Mohican Ping Pong Championships, or the results of the Calcutta Half Marathon. On the air I used to plead with the sports reporter, often the Great Inveraray Bird, to really get their teeth into the thing and give us the results of the Transatlantic Pole Vaulting Finals, Five-a-side Inter-Varsity Conkers Match or better yet, the Nude Hang-Gliding Championships. And then there were the sportsmen who were always 'pulling out their personal bests', and one memorable occasion when 'Daley Thompson really pulled everything out'. Alma ran in the London Marathon once and was in the class called 'Virgin Women'. What? At fifty-five and after two marriages for heaven's sake!

Soon life, as usual, began to imitate art. I saw a Land-Rover and truck parked at Marble Arch once and the logo on the side said 'Alka Seltzer Ballooning Team'. What a gloriously surreal, if slightly indelicate picture this conjured up.

Probably I got most enjoyment out of something called the FA Cup Draw, which Radio 2 broadcast with a sort of religious devotion. As far as I could ascertain, this whole ridiculous rigmarole takes place at Lancaster Gate tube station and consists of a gathering of wise and wizened old men with beards and long white nightshirts. The Grand Vizier and Most High Panjandrum of this tribe always comes armed with a little cloth bag full of balls which he takes devilish delight in jiggling. This ball-jiggling ritual can take many minutes. In the background, the commentator describes the scene in tones of hushed reverence. Suddenly the chief face produces a ball out of the bag and exclaims, 'Accrington Stanley!' at which the commentator whispers 'militant tendency' and then another ball appears 'Corinthian Casuals', which draws the retort, 'woodcraft folk'.

This game can be played for hours until total tedium sets in. The fact that this whole farcical pantomime is presented in such a sombre reverential fashion gives it an added touch of hysteria. Arrogantly, I felt that my version of events was an infinitely more entertaining saga than the real thing ever possibly was.

*   *   *

I always loved peculiar names of people and places; Bryantspuddle, Piddletrenthide and Pratt's Bottom contain intrinsic comic features. It's also something of a mystery as to why Neasden, Goole and Frinton elicit such derisory mirth.

I went to school with an enormous great fat chap called John Clack, of course he was invariably known as Jack Clack. There used to be a TV presenter out in the regions somewhere, his name was Michael Hunt, but who insisted on being known as Mick Hunt, which when pronounced in a certain way sounds very unsavoury indeed. Then there was Cardinal Sin of the Philippines and the Arab oil man, Shake Ya Money and of course our old friend, Dung Show Ping.

'Good evening, Dung. How are things?'

Or perhaps, if he had a TV show, the announcers would say (instead of Wogan, Parkinson, or Harty) 'And now, ladies and gentlemen, let's give a warm welcome to Dung', and the audience would explode into rapturous applause as if the appearance of Dung would constitute a considerable improvement on anything that had gone before.

I met Nelson Riddle a couple of times; he was an enormous great man, well over six feet and powerfully built, and I never quite knew how to address him. 'Nelson' seemed somewhat too chatty and pally and 'Mr Riddle', for a man of that size, just plain silly. I had similar problems with Engelbert Humperdinck:

to call him 'Engelbert' would sound pedantic, and yet to address him as 'Hump' appeared to be a kind of veiled insult.

I used to extract great mileage out of even more arcane territory; sometimes trade names contained great chunks of humour. At home in Liverpool, we had an ancient old toilet which is there to this day and, according to my old cottage-loaf Mum, is functioning better and more often than ever. At the back of the lavatory pan is the inscrutable legend *Shanks, 'The Cecil'*. To take an aristocratic, well-heeled, limp-wristed name like Cecil, and apply it to something as fundamental as a WC takes a perverse form of comic talent. I used to have occasion to pop into a Gents under the road in High Holborn and again the inventive Shanks had been burning the midnight oil and for the high powered, heavy duty urinals which stood like ceramic soldiers awaiting inspection in serried ranks, he gave each one the name 'Dreadnaught'. Shanks was obviously more than ready for anything that nature, or man, could throw at him.

I once heard an apocryphal tale about a Gents in Northampton where all the comfort stations had the assuring title 'Invincible'. Also in the Midlands, I knew of a toilet where the legend on the back of the pan was the 'Beryl'. Obviously some wayward relation of Cecil's. Down in the West Country once we stayed at small hotel and over the toilet in the bathroom was a handwritten note signed The Management, which said, NOTHING WHAT-SOEVER TO BE PUT DOWN THIS WC, which made it seem somewhat pointless to have installed the thing in the first place.

My mother had an old wooden clothes horse for donkey's years and its name on a faded sticky label was the 'Muriel'.

At the BBC there were only ever two types of toilet. The ones for the Executives which were always locked and the ones for the riff-raff which were always blocked.

And some of the people at the BBC had names which betrayed what a warped sense of fun was enjoyed by their parents. There was a Richard Bird, who of course was known as Dickie, and up in Manchester Robert Sleigh, known universally as Bob.

But the BBC seemed to attract people with names whose very sound had a kind of ludicrous correctness about them. I always warmed to a woman called Judith Bumpus; when she was addressed as simply Bumpus, was she flattered or insulted? And then the redoubtable Marlene Pease, where the solemn dignity of Marlene was instantly let down by the trivial wetness of Pease.

And of course, perhaps the greatest of them all, Ellie Updale; whose name I frequently used to take in vain on the air, especially in moments of great stress and emotion and who gave to the language that immortal cry of anguish: 'Who the Ellie Updale?'

* * *

Today is Monday 1st August and I am still here, but the 'I' that is sitting here now is so irrevocably different from the one that existed before. It is difficult to comprehend the sheer totality of the sudden transformation of my life.

Exactly six months ago, I told the BBC that because of the deterioration in my speech, I felt that I could no longer give a fully professional performance and so would have to quit. My memories of those first few hours after the decision are like a Dante's Inferno of painful emotions. Slowly the full horror of what was happening to me began to gnaw away at my mind. It dominated every moment and every thought. Alma and I wept in floods and we began to be almost overwhelmed by unanswerable questions; why cancer? why a cancer on the mouth that prevents me doing the work that was my vocation, my gift? why now? why us? We held each other and cried some more, like two confused, lost children.

Eventually we managed to compose ourselves enough to prepare a meal and have a glass or two of wine, which took the edge off the searing pain and anguish we felt, a sort of sullen numbness settled on us both.

Later that evening, Bryant Marriott, the Controller of Radio 2, rang to say that the BBC would be releasing a press statement about my condition and decision to quit. He said that he would check the wording of it with me the following morning. Friday 29th January eventually dawned and, after a restless troubled night, haunted by nightmares, curiously that very first morning of not being on the air found us both stangely calm and resigned as we busied ourselves through the morning. Approaching mid-day the phone rang and it was Bryant again, who read over the wording of the press statement to be released at 2 pm. He said he would warn all the other presenters and producers beforehand. This was when the full finality of what was happening pierced my heart. So it was real, I'd got cancer, I could no longer work. My beloved career was over. But this time there were no tears, just a terrible icy feeling of desolation.

I stumbled, dazed, down to the Railway Tavern for a pint and, in the event, had three.

Alma was crying when I got back as the force of the cataclysmic turn of events had hit her all over again.

The two o'clock news led the bulletin with the story of my illness and departure from the BBC. I felt oddly distant from it all as though it were a sad story about somebody else.

Not many moments later, the floodgates burst open and the phone began to ring. It was Ken Bruce. I replaced the receiver and the phone rang again. This time it was David Jacobs, who also tearfully expressed his deep shock at the news. All that long afternoon, the phone never stopped ringing. The fact that everyone was so kind and compassionate made it somehow even harder to take.

At about mid-afternoon, as well as the constant phone calls, the front doorbell rang to add its jarring contribution to this emotional torture. A seemingly endless parade of friends, neighbours and even perfect strangers turned up on the doorstep, bearing bunches of flowers, boxes of chocolates and bottles of wine. Again, their kindness brought up the tears.

By teatime, Alma and I were both a gibbering, quivering state of emotional collapse, and we took the phone off the hook. Then I remembered that Lynda Lee-Potter of the *Daily Mail* had promised to ring at 6 pm for the full definitive story of what had happened. I replaced the receiver and immediately the phone rang yet again. This time it was David Hatch, Managing Director of BBC Radio, expressing his sympathy and offering us every support.

It was all a little like being present at your own death.

Lynda eventually got through, she'd been getting the engaged tone for an hour and a half.

At some point during that harrowing evening, two dishevelled reporters from the *Sun* appeared on the doorstep and took photographs of Alma and me, both in tears in the hall. I began to dread what on earth they would print the following day.

By ten o'clock we both could take no more, so I took the phone off the hook and we went to bed, where we both lay awake for most of the night desperately clinging to each other. I suppose sheer emotional exhaustion must have overtaken us in the end because we both awoke suddenly with the front door bell being rung frantically. It was the postman bearing an armful of letters and cards, telemessages and assorted parcels. This healthy crop of about fifty items was just the harbinger of a total wave of post that was to engulf us during the following days, weeks and indeed months.

At about nine that morning I decided I had better replace the phone on the hook. It rang at once – Sandra Chalmers from the BBC Press Office asked me had I seen the morning papers. I said that I hadn't yet. She said she wanted to warn me about the enormous extent of the coverage of my story. Evidently, all the papers carried the story prominently, mostly on the front pages. Again I was overwhelmed by that awful feeling . . . so it's all really true. I wondered if Alma and I would have the courage to go and do the Saturday shopping in the village now that the whole world knew the truth.

The phone continued its incessant ringing all that day, all the calls were from good friends and kind colleagues, all expressing similar tearful emotions. It was just that Alma and I both found the whole thing so totally wearing and mentally draining. One of the calls was more welcome than most, it was our dear friend Malcolm, who casually wondered if I fancied our usual Saturday lunchtime pint. That day it was a million times more welcome than ever, so Alma and I decided to brazen out the stares of the people in the village and a sort of pig-headed defiance came over us. Why on earth should we hide like criminals just because I've got cancer? I am not going to become a hermit and sit cowering in a corner. 'And in any case,' said Alma, 'I want to buy all the papers'.

As we approached the village, in a strange way we both felt relieved that everybody did know. Now there was no longer any need to explain away the big dressing on my chin as being an abscess or the result of an accident. Presumably now, people would no longer ask and simply accept the fact.

Malcolm was already at the bar when we arrived. Beside him was an enormous pile of newspapers, everything from the *Financial Times* to the *Star*, and the story of Alma and me featured prominently in all of them or so she said. I couldn't bear to look at them. Evidently the only paper that didn't run the story was the *Independent*, and I remember feeling vaguely irritated that they should consider our news too trivial to print.

That hour or so in the pub with Malcolm was a glorious release valve for us; for the first time for what seemed an eternity we could let our minds think of something other than the cancer.

When we got back home, the phone was still ringing and continued to do so for the rest of the day and well into the evening.

By now, the spontaneous haemorrhaging was becoming more torrential, prolonged and frequent. Often I would be two hours or more hanging over the bathroom sink with the wound squirting blood like a tap, and then it would stop as suddenly as it had begun and I would feel strangely relieved that the whole frightening rigmarole would be over for a day or so. Even so, whenever I went out, if only down to the village, I would go armed with a bag full of towels just in case. I was also feeling increasingly tired; the walk from the garden, upstairs to the bathroom would leave me weak and exhausted, and as my appetite seemed to have vanished, I began to look increasingly haunted and haggard.

My GP, an understanding boy called Desmond, kept pressing me to undergo a short course of radiotherapy, but I still housed a terrible irrational fear of it. However, I promised Desmond I would think about it. He never used the word 'cure'.

Alma and I were still pressing on with a variety of homeopathic remedies. Every day it seemed we read something or heard something that would mean including another enzyme or vitamin to the dozens I was already taking. We were spending fortunes daily in the health food shop and the chemist. The tumour also had to be cleaned and dressed every morning, and more often if there had been bleeding sessions in between. Alma coped so wonderfully with the sordid routine, she approached the whole thing outwardly with a kind of cheerful stoicism. Inside, her mind was probably in an even bigger state of turmoil than mine was.

I was, in many ways, more depressed about having to stop working than I was about the cancer.

* * *

In the middle of all the maelstrom of emotions we were feeling that weekend, Alma's son David rang up from Manchester and said that he and his wife, Julie, and the baby Paul were keen to book a holiday in the Algarve. He said it would be nice if Alma and I could go with them. It was to be in May for a fortnight. At first this struck me as some kind of sick joke. I felt so wretched physically and mentally that the thought of a holiday abroad was impossible. In any case, the whole idea was academic, it was still only January and by May it was extremely unlikely that I would still be on this earth, let alone the Algarve. However, David was so keen about it he went ahead and booked it. I was certain that as far as I was concerned, it would never happen. I couldn't imagine what state I'd be in in a week's time, let alone in four months.

That first weekend became an exhausted turmoil of phone calls, visitors and arrays of gifts on the doorstep. Alma and I teetered between uncontrollable tears and a kind of depressed numbness. The agony seemed to be never-ending and we longed for some means of escape, but given the unpredictability of the tumour, that was out of the question. It was hardly acceptable socially to be sitting at dinner in a posh hotel and my suddenly bleeding all over the tablecloth.

Financially too there were worries. Although we had never lived up to our income, and had a certain amount in savings, long term prospects were not bright. Being freelance and self-employed meant that if I wasn't working I didn't get paid. I began to depress myself further by trying to work out exactly when the money would run out. The irony was that had I done the decent thing and quickly died, Alma would have been financially very comfortable as we were awash with life insurance. I did have a tiny health insurance but from what I could discover, it would pay out in benefit rather less than the premiums. We seemed to be staring at total disaster on all fronts.

But on the Monday morning, there came two chunks of light in the gloom. Sandy Chalmers rang to say that several national newspapers wanted to print our story and they were offering fairly tidy sums of money for the privilege. In addition, a book publisher who had first approached me a couple of years previously, now more than ever wanted me to write my autobiography. Again, the money involved was significant and would stave off our arrival in the gutter for some months. If both things came to fruition I would end up earning more than I would have done had I been working. God does the oddest things in most peculiar ways.

*   *   *

During that first harrowing week away from the BBC, I didn't dare let the thought enter my mind that my lovely life in broadcasting was over. I was already too near the brink to take on board the fact that I would never again set foot inside Broadcasting House. At this time there was a very real temptation to assuage the anguish by resorting to drink. I succumbed on several occasions during those first few weeks; at one particularly low point, it seemed that the cancer was less likely to get me than cirrhosis of the liver.

Suddenly, on that Monday, we began to be inundated with torrential avalanches of mail, and over the weeks it continued arriving by the sackful. Quite often the post office van would make special deliveries to our house with the sacks of cards, letters and parcels. Soon my office at home resembled Mount Pleasant Sorting Office. As well as all this, the BBC too were being bombarded with post. Many times, Julie at the BBC had to hire vans to transport it here. I surely couldn't cope with this explosive outburst of love, sympathy and support, and far from comforting me, I found a lot of it intensely distressing. It was like reading thousands of versions of my own obituary.

But we did have to sort through it all, as many of the letters contained money, cheques and frequently expensive gift tokens. Everyone simply wanted to express their shock and sadness at what had happened, as though I was a member of their own family who had suffered this fate. But there was more than one letter that even made me laugh in those dark days. I had a note from an old friend, Mike Begg, a TV director with whom I had worked often on various programmes, including many Miss World shows. I knew he was a fan of my work on radio, but until his note arrived I never quite realised just how devoted. It simply said, 'Thanks pal, you really fucked up my weekend!'

*　　*　　*

Alma and I stumbled through those first few days and weeks in a state of confused shock, I felt that we could allow ourselves a day or two of readjustment, it was like suffering the bereavement of the death of a close relation. I was grieving for the loss of my career, a kind of impotent torpor settled on us both, and all the while the phone continued its incessant jangling as we were quickly being buried under the torrents of posts and gifts of flowers and champagne. We cried frequently and unpredictably, an especially kind word or understanding message would set us off again. The cancer was now secondary, just coping from moment to moment was all we could hope to do. Obviously we were approaching a different kind of crisis, not so much medical as emotional and mental. We were both in danger of snapping altogether.

One of the calls that week was from our old friend, Maurice Potter, in whose cottage, buried at the back of beyond in Sussex, I was to write most of my autobiography. He said he would have to be in the City for a meeting the following Monday and could he pop in and maybe go for a spot of lunch; but when he turned up he was dressed in sweater and jeans and I knew that this fictitious meeting in the City was simply a ruse to come and see us. Evidently, quite by coincidence that very morning he had heard about a Healer who lived a couple of villages away from him. The Healer was reported to have had some remarkable successes and so we thought it worth a try to see if the man could conjure up some instant miracle cure for me. I was a little sceptical about the whole idea, but at least it would afford us the chance to spend a couple of days with the Potters. Even if the Healer did no good, then a short break in Sussex away from all the phone calls and letters would in itself be of great value, so we arranged to go down the following week.

*   *   *

At around this time, the *Daily Express* was selected to compile a series of exclusive features about our story. I was extremely reluctant to do this, never having had much sympathy with those who sell their story to Grub Street. But I would now have no income at all apart from the small health insurance, and so money, or a lack of it would at some point become a problem, and the *Daily Express* was offering a not inconsiderable sum. So, against my better judgement, I agreed that we should do it.

The journalist assigned to the job was a lively, understanding woman called Gill Martin, who handled the interview with great sympathy and tact. It can't have been an easy story for her to write. We had three or four sessions with her and the photographer and found the whole thing incredibly exhausting. The mere repetition of the bald facts of what had happened to us was tedious in itself because we were both already going over and over in our minds the recent events. I was also worried as to what sort of sensational 'angle' the newspaper would put on our story, so I had to be careful to watch exactly what I said.

In the event we needn't have worried. Gill's pieces for the

paper were a model of taste and compassion and seemed to be well received generally. As indeed was the money they paid us: at least it would stave off the day when we would have to cope with cancer *and* poverty.

*   *   *

As I wrote earlier, I was approached some years ago by the publishers Constable to write my life story. I was flattered by the offer, of course, but being so busy at the time I did nothing about it. However, after the news broke that I was off the air for good, they contacted me again. This surprised me because I thought that now I was no longer to be a name on the BBC they would lose interest as the story was over. On the contrary, they felt that now there was an even more compelling tale to tell, so again, with one eye on the income this could produce, I agreed to try and write it. They wanted 60,000 words which I imagined to be about the length of the Bible. It seemed an impossible task, but I began to write *Tomorrow is too late*.

*   *   *

My general health by this time was getting worse. The tumour under my chin would bleed profusely and unpredictably for hours on end, which made each moment worrying as I constantly checked the bandage for any tell-tale sign of red, which was a warning that the torrent was about to begin. Socially, this obviously made things difficult and I took to having a bagful of towels with me wherever I went. Eating too, was becoming an increasing problem. My lower teeth were all very loose and even moving my jaw was tiring, so meals became something of an ordeal and I began to eat less and less. I was also starting to get twinges of sudden stabbing pain.

We left for Sussex with an enormous sense of relief. The calm and serenity of the Potters' delightful cottage was bliss indeed after the weeks of constant nagging phone calls at home. We both felt relaxed and peaceful at last. The Healer, Phil Edwards, lived a couple of miles away and ran a sort of Healing Clinic tucked in at the back of his own cottage. Phil, himself, is a tall bulky man with penetrating eyes and a bone-crunching handshake. He was obviously no stranger to the ways of the world. He smoked quite steadily as we talked. He said that he had known already that I would come and see him.

He discussed my former lifestyle and hopes and fears for the future. He said that disease is the direct result of dis-ease. In other words, a troubled conscious state of mind can easily distort the body's own natural healing process and result in a variety of complaints – cancer being one of them. I must try, he said, to cultivate a feeling of inner peace and harmony, which to a natural worrier like me was asking a lot. Eventually, after an hour or so, he ushered me into an inner sanctum. It was a bright, airy room, sparsely furnished with only a couple of upright chairs and a small stool facing the window. The warm sunshine of that spring morning filled the room with a kind of vivid radiance, and it was so quiet it was almost possible to hear the silence.

Phil invited me to sit on the stool facing the window. On the sill was a glass paperweight inside which was a miniature rose. He told me to look at the rose and think of nothing else, to empty my mind of everything, to forget all fears, plans, worries and just concentrate on the rose. He asked me how long it had been since I simply sat still and was at peace.

'I can't remember ever doing that,' I said.

He moved behind me and said nothing more. After a while my eyes closed and I heard a lovely soft string orchestra start playing. Phil began by putting his hands on my shoulders and then almost imperceptibly, his hands started fluttering gently

[156]

around my head and neck and around the tumour itself. I was calm and at ease with the music, the warmth of the sunshine and Phil's hands moving gently around my face. I could feel the tensions of the previous months falling away from my mind.

After perhaps forty minutes or so, the session ended or rather just faded away into silence. I sat there for a while, just relishing the serenity of the moment.

I went out and rejoined Alma, Joan and Maurice in the car. I was weepy, in a happy sort of way, even if the healing didn't work it had certainly relieved that awful apprehension and given me a measure of peace. It had also given me a towering thirst, so we all went off to one of those delightful Sussex country pubs nearby. King and Barnes never tasted better.

Joan and Maurice drove us back to Blackheath. As I approached our front door I could hear the phone ringing. It seemed like an obscene intrusion and brutal end to an idyllic interval. Joan and Maurice sat in the kitchen drinking coffee as Alma and I took turns answering the phone which rang constantly. After half an hour of this bedlam, all the pressure had returned and we seemed to be back emotionally where we started. Sussex seemed like a million miles away, a cruel dream snatched away from us. We were once again in the teeth of the nightmare.

The calls were all from sincere and well-meaning people who simply wanted to express their sympathy and to offer us help in any way they could; friends, colleagues, passing acquaintances, long-lost distant cousins all rang to tell of their shock at the news. It was just that the calls were continuous. They became a gnawing, nagging reminder of my condition every waking moment.

Not that the cancer was easy to forget anyway, night or day. It was like a great black iron fist dominating every corner of our minds. We felt totally swamped by the obsession. Alma was able to cope with it all far more strongly than I could. By now, not eating or sleeping properly and with the enormous loss of blood, I began to feel really ill. I was constantly weary and frequently lapsed into hours of weeping and self-pity, which depressed us both still further. The situation was obviously approaching some kind of catharsis.

*   *   *

The crisis happened one morning in February. I had woken up feeling even more weary than ever, but stumbled through the chores of the day by summoning up what little reserves of energy I could. After a bath and a shave, I had to go and lie down again for half an hour. Later in the kitchen during breakfast, I began to feel very quivery and lightheaded. Suddenly everything went black and I keeled off the chair like a felled ox.

Eventually, when I came round, there were the faces of four men and a woman looking down at me lying on the floor. I became aware of a hushed muttering as the faces peered at me. The faces slowly came into focus and I recognised Alma, my GP Desmond, and three men in uniforms who, it turned out, were ambulancemen. They gave me a glass of water and I started feeling stronger. Alma said that I had gone a peculiar shade of green and she thought that I was going to expire there and then.

After a while, they manhandled me upstairs and I lay on the bed shivering, shrouded in towels and blankets. I slowly fell into a fitful troubled sleep.

In the afternoon Desmond returned and said that the collapse was entirely due to the enormous quantities of blood I had been losing. He said he could arrange for a blood transfusion, but we both agreed that it would be silly to start pumping blood in at one end only for it to come pouring out of the other end. The other question was what Desmond referred to as 'a short burst of sunshine' – radiation. This, he hoped, would have the effect of cauterizing the tumour and stopping the bleeding for a time. It is difficult to explain the irrational fear that radiation evokes in me. I picture an enormous shiny cigar tube with me entombed inside it, and the lethal rays frying my guts. I imagine the fearful power of Chernobyl being unleashed on me. It all seems insidiously frightening. The radiation is so strong and penetrating and yet its presence is impossible to detect by normal human senses. I felt that something that could wreak the havoc that was caused at Hiroshima, with the after-effects still being felt today, could only do great harm. If it was all so benevolent, why did the radiologists have to hide behind thick lead screens to administer it? During the past couple of years, two of our close friends, both suffering from bone cancer, underwent the full course of radiotherapy and endured the hideous side-effects, only to die slow and painful deaths in the end. It seemed such a medieval method of treatment.

So I was faced with a bitterly cruel dilemma. Either I carried on losing blood alarmingly, or I could submit myself to something I'd always feared. In the end I decided that my life was no longer very dignified anyway, constantly shrouded in towels and fearful of going anywhere in case the tumour suddenly started erupting again, so I agreed to see a consultant at University College Hospital.

Even the words over the door filled me with profound horror, 'Department of Radiotherapy'. Had Alma not been there by my side, I would have turned and fled. The consultant was a kindly, understanding man who explained that he could give me a very low dose of radiation which would have few of the inhuman side-effects and yet would help make the tumour behave itself for a while. He offered to show me the machine.

With great trepidation we stepped inside a small room. Suspended from the ceiling was a circular, shallow cylinder about two feet across. It was not quite the satanic machine I'd imagined, although I was still consumed by an awful dread, but I was eventually persuaded that I should try a test run to see how it felt. It would last four minutes.

I lay on the bed as the radiologist focused the machine about eighteen inches above the tumour. I heard the heavy lead door slam shut with an ominous finality. Four minutes. I was literally rigid with fear, so to help ease my mind a little, I recited the Creed to myself, over and over again. I was terrified in case the radiologist would get distracted and forget about me and I would overcook. I imagined myself finally emerging as a shrunken, blackened sausage.

*　　*　　*

OCTOBER 19TH, 1988

It is just such a blissfully, mild, Indian summer's day; as I sat on the heath, autumn bathed me in its warm sunshine and I found it hard to acknowledge the appalling future that faces me. It seems that my condition is getting quite rapidly worse, and I view the next days and months (maybe) with a kind of cosmic dread. The fact of dying is less of a problem than the manner of it. Even if I knew quite what was going to happen, it would not ease that oppressing feeling of foreboding.

I can now make only barely intelligible conversation, with much spitting and spluttering. In the Post Office yesterday, trying to order sixteen self-employment insurance stamps was an almost insurmountable burden, which left the clerk almost hoarse from bellowing 'Beg your pardon?'!

And the glass partition speckled with spit – an exercise I shan't trouble to repeat. The DHSS can go hang! My face is now badly swollen and distended, especially first thing in the mornings when frequently, like this morning, my right eye is completely closed. When I got up today with bloated cheeks and ashen pallor, I looked like a monstrous caricature of the face I had looked at for forty-six years. I really looked like somebody else, some mutant thing that couldn't possibly poke its nose out of the door for fear of frightening the horses and children.

The dressing which Alma is now having to do three times a day is getting larger every time as the cancer spreads down into my neck and throat. I used to joke lightheartedly about turning into the Phantom of the Opera, and yet now it appears to be becoming hideously true. The day, I suppose, will dawn soon when I will no longer be able to spend a happy hour in the pub with Graham and Alma (which we did today).

The pain has also now become more determined in its hold on me. Great jabbing knives shoot up through my jaw, I physically wince at its power and force. It seems to drain me of all energy and resolve.

There is, in addition, a bit of a growing problem in swallowing. My tongue seems to be glued down to the floor of my mouth and so even taking drinks, let alone food and tablets ain't easy. It often takes two or three goes to down a painkiller.

I'm beginning to get seriously depressed about it all and wonder at the loving nature of our caring God. All the things I loved in all the world are slowly being taken from me; conversation, the conviviality of a meal out in a restaurant, long walks in the country or by the sea, are now all just mordant memories. It still feels as if I'm being punished for some galactic sin I have committed.

We've just had a glorious fortnight with Joan and Maurice in a tumbled down fisherman's cottage in Land's End, where the gales blew in and the rain lashed down, superb weather in God's own country. And yet not to be able to walk with the dog up the sandhills and on the rocks and be imprisoned by weakness and fear in the cottage seemed a cruel way to rub salt in to the wound. Often at lunchtimes, I used to manage to totter the few hundred yards along the dunes to the pub in Sennen Cove called the Old Success. I would sit there weak and terminally weary, as I quaffed the pints of Bass and contemplated the herculean feat of getting back to the cottage. Sitting down, too, is a bit of a painful exercise. I have lost so much weight now that the bones in my bottom need half a ton of heavy duty cushioning.

On our return to Cherry Cottage, we discovered that my book was number one in the *Sunday Times* charts and so obviously champagne was called for. But even that seemed to burn my mouth. It was bitter and acid. One of my greatest joys in life – a glass of rosé champagne – has now turned to wormwood and gall. No more the days of wine and roses. It is a bit like watching yourself dying. On second thoughts, it is *exactly* that.

* * *

Throughout all this ridiculous episode, Alma has sustained me beyond measure. Apart from having to gawp at the wretched cancer itself three times a day, she maintains a beautiful, stoic cheerfulness about it all. Quite how, I will never know. Occasionally, the mask slips for both of us. When we got back from Cornwall on Monday, we were both overwhelmed by tears. It was not sadness at being home, just a sense that we both knew somehow that it could never be repeated. The next time there would be one person missing.

Alma is spending her life doing the washing. I can no longer swallow saliva unconsciously, and so in the night my mouth dribbles a revolting cocktail of blood and spit all over the sheets and pillowcases. It also stinks quite revoltingly, so the next morning there is yet another great heap of pyjama jackets and bed linen to attack.

Radio Manchester rang up this morning to ask my permission (!) to hold a Bog-Eyed Jog there next month for Children in Need. It all brought back floods of memories of those glorious days out in various windswept stadiums around the country with Denis, Graham, Julie and Alma; standing about in the pouring rain in the pitch dark and doing ridiculous live radio shows. It is incomprehensible that this time last year under the beard the tumour was barely discernible. It dripped a noxious liquid from time to time, but apart from that I was as fit as an ox. And now, in such a short, fleeting time, my life has changed beyond all recognition.

No longer am I able to order a 'natural orange' for Alma because I can't pronounce it. Restaurants are a thing of the past. I can't chew the food. Walking up the hill from the village leaves me puffing and panting on a bench near the Hare and Billet. As I say, because I am mentally still alert, I am watching with increasing horror my own deterioration and eventually, I suppose, death. It is a torture of the most intense kind.

Occasionally, the thought occurs to me to hasten the end. What would be the point of blood transfusions, intravenous feeding and constant nursing if the result eventually were the same?

*   *   *

NOVEMBER 14TH, 1988

Things are now moving on apace and not altogether in the right direction. I seem to be heading for the brink quite quickly. My face is now so swollen that it is often a matter of serious debate whether I go out at all. I am permanently tired and more frequently depressed.

On Thursday we are due to go to Manchester for the Children in Need Bog-Eyed Jog. I long not to have to go, mainly because of the effort of having to talk and attempt some kind of jollity in front of David and Julie. Alma could go and do the event, representing me, and I could arrange for the nurse to come and do the dressings while she was away. And if the dressings looked too unsightly to venture forth into the world, then I would stay indoors for a couple of days. No problem.

Except that that is being so selfish. Alma, and indeed I desperately want to see David and Julie and the baby, and if I didn't go to Manchester, Alma would be even more alone and isolated from all she loves most dearly.

In the event we reached a strange, uneven compromise. I felt I couldn't face the journey and all the people, so we agreed that Alma would go up on Thursday, do the gig on Friday and come home that evening.

Brained by Kleenex kitchen tissue in shop. The sudden scramble out of the Railway at a minute appearance of blood on the dressing. It was the shortest time I spent in a pub, two sips of beer and then a headlong dash home through the village. In the event it wasn't blood at all, simply a bit of old matter falling away on to the gauze, but appearing somewhat alarming. Not so long ago I would have popped back to the Railway, but now it didn't seem important.

*　　*　　*

JANUARY 1ST, 1989
New Year's Day. What an astonishing fact. It just seems beyond my belief that I could have come so far, and still be here in such a comparative state of being okay.

Epilogue

There are so many stages of mourning and anybody who is bereaved has to go through them all. Initially there's shock and numbness and then you go through a period of fantasy when you can't actually comprehend that the person you love is really dead. The third stage comes when you accept the reality of loss and this often releases an outpouring of intense grief. The next stage is having to come to terms with painful memories, going to places where you both went, seeing people you always saw together. It's also very important to remember the person who died as they really were, not to put them on some kind of pedestal.

Ray and I were the closest of friends as well as lovers and I miss not having my friend around. I miss the ordinary, chatty, silly things. There's nobody to laugh with. I don't laugh like I used to. I feel one legged. I miss lying in bed, looking out over the open heath through the half closed curtains, waiting for the sound of Ray's footsteps on the creaking stairs. I miss his lovely bog-eyed face peering round the door and a fine brew of tea in my favourite mug. That was always my treasured moment of the day when Ray would give me the first kiss. Now if I don't go out I never talk to anybody, which is true of anybody who's lost their partner when there are no children. Everytime I walk back into the house I always say, 'Hello Ray, I'm back'.

But there have been good times since Ray died. I'll walk across the heath and suddenly know I feel smashing, alive and it's good to realise that. I think that now I'm more aware of the happy moments, they really do register. I've felt desolate at times, and angry and lonely but I've never felt defeated.

I was so blessed to be married to Ray.

Acknowledgements

I would like to thank Harry and Win Read and Derrik and Betty Tribble for their prayers, their love and their guidance

And thanks too to Julie Pearce who faithfully typed out Ray's manuscript.

My thanks to Lynda Lee-Potter for her foreword to my book and also for her encouragement and confidence in me.

Finally, my heartfelt thanks to my son David and his wife Julie for the very special love they showered on Ray and me and continue to do so.

THE RAY MOORE TRUST

The Ray Moore Trust has been established in memory of this popular BBC Radio 2 broadcaster.

The Trust, which is a charity, has already initiated and is maintaining bursaries known as 'The Ray Moore Bursaries' at the Royal Northern College of Music, Manchester.

These bursaries will be awarded to talented students (under the age of 25), who through their own efforts have qualified for entrance to the College but haven't the necessary financial resources available to undertake four years at college. The Trust will guarantee them support for the complete course.

Further details regarding donations and covenants from:

The Ray Moore Trust
Barclays Bank PLC
74/75 East Street
Chichester, West Sussex
PO19 1HR

Bestselling Non-Fiction

☐	Complete Hip and Thigh Diet	Rosemary Conley	£2.99
☐	Staying off the Beaten Track	Elizabeth Gundrey	£6.99
☐	Raw Energy: Recipes	Leslie Kenton	£3.99
☐	The PM System	Dr J A Muir Gray	£5.99
☐	Women Who Love Too Much	Robin Norwood	£3.50
☐	Letters From Women Who Love Too Much	Robin Norwood	£3.50
☐	Fat is a Feminist Issue	Susie Orbach	£2.99
☐	Callanetics	Callan Pinckney	£6.99
☐	Elvis and Me	Priscilla Presley	£3.50
☐	Love, Medicine and Miracles	Bernie Siegel	£3.50
☐	Communion	Whitley Strieber	£3.50
☐	Trump: The Art of the Deal	Donald Trump	£3.99

Prices and other details are liable to change

ARROW BOOKS, BOOKSERVICE BY POST, PO BOX 29, DOUGLAS, ISLE OF MAN, BRITISH ISLES

NAME..

ADDRESS...

....

....

Please enclose a cheque or postal order made out to Arrow Books Ltd. for the amount due and allow the following for postage and packing.

U.K. CUSTOMERS: Please allow 22p per book to a maximum of £3.00.

B.F.P.O. & EIRE: Please allow 22p per book to a maximum of £3.00.

OVERSEAS CUSTOMERS: Please allow 22p per book.

Whilst every effort is made to keep prices low it is sometimes necessary to increase cover prices at short notice. Arrow Books reserve the right to show new retail prices on covers which may differ from those previously advertised in the text or elsewhere.

A Selection of Arrow Books

☐	No Enemy But Time	Evelyn Anthony	£2.95
☐	The Lilac Bus	Maeve Binchy	£2.99
☐	Rates of Exchange	Malcolm Bradbury	£3.50
☐	Prime Time	Joan Collins	£3.50
☐	Rosemary Conley's Complete Hip and Thigh Diet	Rosemary Conley	£2.99
☐	Staying Off the Beaten Track	Elizabeth Gundrey	£6.99
☐	Duncton Wood	William Horwood	£4.50
☐	Duncton Quest	William Horwood	£4.50
☐	A World Apart	Marie Joseph	£3.50
☐	Erin's Child	Sheelagh Kelly	£3.99
☐	Colours Aloft	Alexander Kent	£2.99
☐	Gondar	Nicholas Luard	£4.50
☐	The Ladies of Missalonghi	Colleen McCullough	£2.50
☐	The Veiled One	Ruth Rendell	£3.50
☐	Sarum	Edward Rutherfurd	£4.99
☐	Communion	Whitley Strieber	£3.99

Prices and other details are liable to change

ARROW BOOKS, BOOKSERVICE BY POST, PO BOX 29, DOUGLAS, ISLE OF MAN, BRITISH ISLES

NAME...

ADDRESS...

....

....

Please enclose a cheque or postal order made out to Arrow Books Ltd. for the amount due and allow the following for postage and packing.

U.K. CUSTOMERS: Please allow 22p per book to a maximum of £3.00.

B.F.P.O. & EIRE: Please allow 22p per book to a maximum of £3.00.

OVERSEAS CUSTOMERS: Please allow 22p per book.

Whilst every effort is made to keep prices low it is sometimes necessary to increase cover prices at short notice. Arrow Books reserve the right to show new retail prices on covers which may differ from those previously advertised in the text or elsewhere.

Arrow Health

☐ The Alexander Principle	Wilfred Barlow	£2.95
☐ The Zinc Solution	D. Bryce-Smith	£3.50
☐ Goodbye to Arthritis	Patricia Byrivers	£2.95
☐ Rosemary Conley's Complete Hip and Thigh Diet	Rosemary Conley	£2.99
☐ No Change	Wendy Cooper	£2.99
☐ Day Light Robbery	Dr Damien Downing	£3.99
☐ The Biogenic Diet	Leslie Kenton	£3.99
☐ Ageless Ageing: The Natural Way to Stay Young	Leslie Kenton	£3.95
☐ Raw Energy: Recipes	Leslie Kenton	£3.99
☐ Joy of Beauty	Leslie Kenton	£6.99
☐ Sexual Cystitis	Angela Kilmartin	£3.99
☐ PM System: Preventive Medicine For Total Health	Dr J A Muir Gray	£5.99
☐ Women Who Love Too Much	Robin Norwood	£3.50
☐ Fat is a Feminist Issue	Susie Orbach	£2.99
☐ Callanetics	Callan Pinckney	£6.99
☐ Love, Medicine and Miracles	Bernie Siegel	£3.50

Prices and other details are liable to change

ARROW BOOKS, BOOKSERVICE BY POST, PO BOX 29, DOUGLAS, ISLE OF MAN, BRITISH ISLES

NAME...

ADDRESS...

....

....

Please enclose a cheque or postal order made out to Arrow Books Ltd. for the amount due and allow the following for postage and packing.

U.K. CUSTOMERS: Please allow 22p per book to a maximum of £3.00.

B.F.P.O. & EIRE: Please allow 22p per book to a maximum of £3.00.

OVERSEAS CUSTOMERS: Please allow 22p per book.

Whilst every effort is made to keep prices low it is sometimes necessary to increase cover prices at short notice. Arrow Books reserve the right to show new retail prices on covers which may differ from those previously advertised in the text or elsewhere.